Under Grace

By Fred DeRuvo

STUDY-GROW-KNOW
MINISTRIES
← Studying to Grow through Knowledge of God's Word! →
WWW.STUDYGROWKNOW.COM

Published in Scotts Valley, California, by Study-Grow-Know
www.studygrowknow.com • www.studygrowknow.tv • www.studygrowknowblog.com

Unless noted, Scripture quotations are from the New American Standard Bible, Copyright ©1960, 1962, 1963, 1968, 1971, 1972, 1973, 1975, 1977, 1995 by The Lockman Foundation.

Cover design by Fred DeRuvo

All images unless otherwise noted were created by Fred DeRuvo

Cover Image: © Iakov Kalinin - Fotolia.com

Oneplace.com logo is a registered trademark of Oneplace.com – used with permission.

Edited by: Hannah Richards

Library of Congress Cataloging-in-Publication Data

DeRuvo, Fred, 1957 –

ISBN 0983700648
EAN-13 9780983700647

1. Religion – Christian Theology – Soteriology

Contents

Foreword: 5

Chapter 1:   Future Sins: Forgiven or Not?... 7

Chapter 2:   Lordship Salvation: Right or Wrong?............................ 20

Chapter 3:   Claiming vs. Being 31

Chapter 4:   The Prodigal Son 35

Chapter 5:   Unmerited Favor 57

Chapter 6:   The Older Son... 66

Chapter 7:   He Saw, Agreed, and Changed 79

Chapter 8:   The Father's Unfailing Love.. 89

Chapter 9:   No More Condemnation 102

Chapter 10: The End 120

"Therefore there is now no condemnation for those who are in Christ Jesus."

– Romans 8:1 (NASB)

Foreword

What a topic this is to discuss! It's complicated to say the least and causes people to not only take sides, but it is not long before the name-calling begins in earnest.

On one hand, we have those who believe that unless the Lord is truly permitted to be Lord over one's life all the time, the salvation that the individual enjoys is in danger of being lost. While this might not happen instantaneously, it can be the ultimate consequence of failing to submit your life to the Lord on a constant basis.

On the other hand, we have people who believe that salvation can never be lost and that salvation and His Lordship are permanently intertwined. Yes, it is the Christian's obligation to submit to the Lord, but these folks believe that while we cooperate with the Lord in this endeavor it is the Lord Himself who carries the bulk of the responsibility in making this happen.

Who is right? Wow, that's a zinger, isn't it? We all know that people on both sides of the subject often use the same Scripture to support their opposing viewpoints. One can only wonder how that happens. It is due to the fact that the same *meanings* are not applied to the same words utilized, and we will spend a bit of time going over that. For instance, what does the word "repentance" mean according to Scripture? It's important to know that before we get too deeply into the subject. But even there, people will disagree over the meaning of that word.

To the Lordship Salvation people, repentance means feeling terrible about your sin and therefore yourself. Without this guilt, there is no real repentance. Others who stand opposed to this view take repentance to mean simply turning away from the sin that has bound and kept us servants to sin and SELF. Who is correct? We'll take some time to go over that and you can decide for yourself.

I realize that many, *many* books have been written on this subject and I am not writing this to intend it to be the be-all, end-all. It's *not* the final word. Others may come along and add things to both sides of the issue, hopefully making it even clearer than I have done herein.

My ultimate hope is that this book prompts you to do your own research, and I pray that you start and end with the Bible. I understand the Bible one way and you might understand it another. The reality is that we both need to understand it the way God intended it to be understood.

I would like to be able to say that everything I believe about God and His Word is on par with God's meaning. I simply can't be that sure (or arrogant) about it, so I approach His Word with fear and trepidation, knowing that I am reading His Words, and because of that, I need to grasp His meaning.

I'm not trying to present to you a book that is the truth. I hope it turns out to be that, but I am simply trying to present to you a book that I believe mirrors what God's Word teaches. In the end, I'll let you be the judge, but please understand that it is not my desire to hijack God's Word or His meaning. It is my conscious desire to determine what God's meaning is in His Word. That's all I ever want to do. So, to that end, may you be blessed as you read this and ultimately, more than anything, may the Lord be glorified.

Fred DeRuvo, September 2011

Chapter 1

Future Sins: Forgiven or Not?

"He made you alive together with Him, having forgiven us all our transgressions" - Colossians 2:13b

Not long ago, I read an article in which an author made the statement that not only are the sins in our future *not* automatically forgiven (the ones we have not yet committed), but to hold to such a view is blasphemy (my paraphrase). I was a bit dumbfounded because I have always understood that my sin – all of it – past, present, and future, was dealt with at the cross.

I have long understood that there are people who do not believe in unconditional eternal security, meaning they stand in opposition to the *"once saved, always saved"* doctrine. I guess what I had not considered was the idea that I have future sins that God's forgiveness does not cover until I get there.

God, because of who He is, sees the beginning from the end and the end from the beginning. Because He is God, He is perfectly able and capable of seeing all of this at the same time, as difficult as that may be for us to comprehend.

In my life, I cannot see the end from the beginning, unless we are simply talking about a piece of my life that is already in the past. Of course then it is clearly visible. God goes way beyond this. Not only does He see the beginning from the end of every person's life, but He sees every decision I've ever made and sees what would have happened had I chosen another path or direction rather than the one I did choose.

In truth, God sees every aspect of my life from the very second I was born until I exhale my very last breath all at the same time because all of my life is always in His present tense. If then we are talking about future sins that are allegedly not automatically forgiven (presumably until I get there and actually commit the sin), please consider that while there is a future for me, there is no future for God because He is always in the present. Does this make sense to you? If not, it's likely because I have not explained it well enough. Please bear with me.

I took some time to cruise the Internet searching this subject out, and it is amazing how many times I came across people who believe that the Christian's future sins are not automatically forgiven. This belief is usually held by those who also do not believe in eternal security. Of course, they would say they do believe in eternal security, but that they do not believe in unconditional eternal security. The problem, of course, is that either *"eternal"* means just that or it means something else, something that falls short of actually being eternal.

In that case, Jesus applied a different meaning from what we know as eternal.

So on one hand, there are those who believe that my future sins are not already forgiven and I can conceivably lose my salvation, and on the other hand, there are those like myself who believe that every sin I have ever committed or will ever commit were not only seen by Jesus but taken into account as He died on the cross. There is nothing in my life that is hidden from God and there are too many Scriptures in support of that truth.

Here's the problem, as far as I see it. If a person believes in the idea that my sins – all of them – were not automatically forgiven the day I received Jesus as Savior, what Christians have then is really conditional salvation. It can't be understood in any other way, at least the way I see their position.

This is not to say that people who believe that my future sins are not automatically forgiven believe that salvation can be lost easily. It means that they believe that over time, if a Christian does not regularly confess (or repent of) sins they commit in their life, they will initially lose fellowship with God, and if they remain on that path, will finally lose salvation. They will, in effect, become unborn again and will revert back to the time when they were not "saved." The Holy Spirit's seal referenced by Paul means nothing in that case.

While they might argue that this is an oversimplification of their belief, this is really it in a nutshell. Certainly, they claim they do believe in eternal salvation, but they would also have to admit that this eternal salvation in which they believe is really a form of conditional salvation. In other words, as long as they continue to do the right things (in this case, repent of, confess sin, and ask for forgiveness), their salvation is secure. Apart from this, they do not enjoy eternal salvation at all, in spite of their arguments to the contrary. Some have stated that there is no way to actually know whether you have salvation until after you leave this life.

Admittedly, this is a very difficult subject because people are vehement about what they believe. They draw the line in the sand and will fight to the death over this particular doctrine, it seems. Why shouldn't they, because the doctrine of eternal security of the believer is the basis of Christianity. Either we have it and cannot add to it in any way, shape, or form or we only have it when we add to it through confession and repentance.

Before I go any further, let me say right now and without equivocation that I do not believe Christians should ever have a cavalier attitude with respect to sin. I fully believe that my sin – whenever I am made aware of it – should be immediately and sincerely confessed to the Lord. I also believe that whenever possible, reparations should be made if I have sinned against another person. That may include something as simple as a heartfelt apology or something else, depending upon what I have done. Sin should never be dealt with lightly and certainly never overlooked. But what we are talking about is whether or not the sins I will commit in my future are automatically forgiven by God.

If they are not, then the only sins that were forgiven when I received Jesus were the ones in my past (and present, if I had conceivably sinned while receiving Him as Savior and Lord) and those in my past that I have confessed since then. Is this what the Scriptures teach? Well, you and I both know that people on both sides of the aisle use Scripture to prove their position, don't they? I can take Scripture and use it to assess and prove my point, and someone on the other side of the fence can use the same Scripture to assess and prove their point. How can we know for sure? This is where a bit of fear and trepidation comes into play. Just as I should never be cavalier about sin, I should never be cavalier about His Word and my interpretation or understanding of it. I should always approach His Word with the utmost reverence.

Let's see if I can't sort my way through this subject. Again, we are going to start with the idea that God is outside time. He is not governed by time as I am. He is not limited by time as I am. To Him, my entire life is always in His present tense. There is nothing in my life that He doesn't see until it unfolds. It is all laid bare at the same time. That much we know.

Think about something. If my future sins are not forgiven until I get there, then as soon as I commit a future sin, it is already in my past. The argument then becomes, does God's forgiveness extend to my future sins, or does His forgiveness extend only to my future sins when they become my past sins, or are none of my future sins forgiven (even after they've been committed) until I commit and confess them to Him?

As I stated, I believe that it is my responsibility to confess my sins as I realize them, but I obviously cannot realize that I have committed a "future" sin until it becomes a "past" sin. If I fail to confess that future-turned-past sin, am I in danger of eventually losing my salvation? That is really the key question, as far as I can tell.

I am guessing that there are sins in my future. I have not lived them yet and I don't know what they are going to be, but I know that since I am not perfect because the sin nature still resides within me, I will likely commit future sins. As I sit here composing this article, I am not aware of any past sins that need confession. As far as I can tell, I am right with God. I can think about past sins, the ones God says He does not remember, but I cannot go into the future and "*borrow*" sins by contemplating the sins I might/will commit. If I do, then in effect, those sins are momentarily in the present, and then go into the past. It is almost as if future sins are theoretical. In theory, I will commit future sins, but as soon as I do, they become sins of my past, yet they are always in God's present. Again, this is not to minimize sin at all. It is to attempt to put things in their proper perspective.

The big question here, then, is does the redemption I have through Jesus forgive all my sins, or does it only forgive sins in my present (a misnomer) and past? That is the key question that needs to be answered, so let's see what the Bible says.

Let's first look at Colossians 2:13-15. *"When you were dead in your transgressions and the uncircumcision of your flesh, **He made you alive together with Him**, **having forgiven us all our transgressions**, having canceled out the certificate of debt consisting of decrees against us, which was hostile to us; and He has taken it out of the way, having nailed it to the cross. When He had disarmed the rulers and authorities, He made a public display of them, having triumphed over them through Him."* I have emphasized part of it, as you can see, because it is important.

Paul is telling the Colossian believers (and all believers by default) that:

1. *I was dead because of my sin*
2. *I have been made alive in Jesus*
3. *All my sins have been forgiven*

God wiped out the written law that serves to identify our sins because it was completely fulfilled by Jesus (nailed it to the cross).

Paul is really comparing two things here. He is comparing what I was to what I am now. I was dead, but now I am alive in Christ. Before I came to know Jesus, my sins were unforgiven, but now that I am in Christ, my sins are forgiven. This certainly seems to say to me that all of my sins are forgiven. That would include every sin in my life, whether they are sins of my past or any future sins. Once again, the responsibility of each believer is to confess known sin as soon as we realize we have sinned. But Paul seems to be saying that God's forgiveness covers all of my sin.

This next part is very important, and it required a bit of word searching discovering meaning. Notice Paul uses the phrase, "*being dead.*" That word "*being*" as used by Paul is the participle of "*to be,*" which shows a continuous state of being. In other words, Paul is saying that we were in a continuous state of death prior to receiving salvation. You get that, right? It makes sense. Apart from Jesus, we are continually dead because our sin has made us that way and keeps us that way.

Paul then tells us that something far greater exists than our sin which has made us and keeps us dead. He speaks of our being made alive. That "*something*" is forgiveness. In other words, and this is the really cool part, the phrase "*he has made alive*" is essentially one word in the Greek text. It is an aorist active indicative verb. Yeah, I know, who cares, right? Let's understand though – regardless of what it's called – that it means that Jesus did His work one time and that one time was enough to cover all sin as an ongoing aspect of my salvation. You remember the words "*It is finished*" that Jesus spoke from the cross? What He meant was that He accomplished what was necessary, once for all, in order that our sins – all of them – would be forgiven when we receive Him as Savior and Lord.

Equally important is the use of the word "*having*" by Paul. These are aorist participles, meaning that they are done deals. They have been accomplished. So when Paul says, "having forgiven you all trespasses," he is saying that when we received Jesus and the salvation He and He alone offers, His forgiveness is applied to our lives, which means that "*all trespasses*" have been forgiven – every sin we will ever commit.

Understandably, this line of thinking can lead to a life of licentiousness if misunderstood, and I have a sneaking suspicion that this is why some people don't like it. In effect, they believe that this leads to a life of sinning freely and even encouraging others to do so as the natural consequence of thinking that all of my sins, past, present, and future are forgiven. However, I fully disagree. It is not a natural consequence of thinking this way. It is an unnatural consequence of thinking this way.

The people who say they are Christians and continue to live as if they are not really can't be authentic Christians, can they? That lifestyle does not seem supportable by Scripture. James speaks about it, as does Paul and John in his short epistles.

Some people seem to think that since Christians are no longer condemned (Romans 8) we can live any way we want to live. Though this attitude is incorrect, it does not negate the truth of the doctrine of (unconditional) eternal security. What it *does* do is prove that they have misunderstood the application of that truth to their lives if they are living licentiously.

A person who is authentically saved will not want to sin. They will not think to themselves that they are saved and will go to heaven when they die, so they can live like the devil now.

Paul tells me that I am sealed with the Holy Spirit. *"And do not grieve the Holy Spirit of God, by whom you were sealed for the day of redemption"* (Ephesians 4:30). He also tells me this interesting fact: *"But you are not in the flesh but in the Spirit, if indeed the Spirit of God dwells in you. Now if anyone does not have the Spirit of Christ, he is not His"* (Romans 8:9).

I have read articles by folks who believe that while we are sealed, apparently we are strong enough (through self-will) to actually break that seal. They take passages like John 10:28 – *"and I give eternal life to them, and they will never perish; and no one will snatch them out of My hand"* – and wind up adding to that by saying that while no one can snatch me out of His hand, I can exercise free will and leave. I would strongly disagree, unless of course we believe that God will simply sit back and allow us to walk away. In that case, what is the purpose of being sealed? Is my free will (such as it is) strong enough to break God's seal? I don't think so...

We can also point to passages like the one in Isaiah 43:25, which states, "*I, even I, am the one who wipes out your transgressions for My own sake, And I will not remember your sins.*" Of course, someone will come along and say, that's true, but those are sins in the past. But haven't we established that my entire life is in God's present? How can there be a past or a future where God is concerned? There is only a past and a future where we are concerned.

We could almost argue that the people who think that eternal security is conditional have a problem with pride. Think about it. They believe they can and are actually helping God maintain their salvation.

When they sin, they probably look and act as if they have eaten a bowl of lemons. These people are often extremely rigid, yet they see their rigidity as holiness. They believe when they stand before God He will pat them on the head and tell them how marvelous they are and how tremendous they were in this life that they worked so hard to maintain their salvation. Those same people will look back pitifully at others who did not work as hard as they did to maintain their salvation and possibly even lost it, but were not aware that they did so until the afterlife.

Pride is a very tricky thing. We condemn the beliefs of people in cults because we believe they are adding to Scriptures. Our heart goes out to them personally because they believe, in some measure, that they must earn their salvation. We don't earn our salvation, yet what of the people who believe that they must work to maintain it and if they fail to maintain it, they could possibly lose it? Isn't that the same thing as earning it? I believe it is…

1 John 1:7 tells us, "*But if we walk in the Light as He Himself is in the Light, we have fellowship with one another, and the blood of Jesus His Son cleanses us from all sin.*"

Ephesians 1:7 says, "*In Him we have redemption through His blood, the forgiveness of our trespasses, according to the riches of His grace.*"

I'm aware that John's verse uses the word "*if*" as though that makes it conditional. In reality, John is saying "as" we walk in the Light, because we just learned from Ephesians 4:30 and Romans 8:9 that I am sealed by the Holy Spirit and I no longer live in the flesh. If I no longer live in the flesh, while this does not mean I will never sin again, it means I obviously am in fellowship with God. Why? Because since I have received salvation from the Lord, "*the blood of Jesus His Son cleanses [me] from all sin.*" John says, "*all sin.*" God's forgiveness is uniformly applied to the entirety of my life, once for all.

Those who repudiate unconditional eternal security use passages like 1 John 1:9, which says, "*If we confess our sins, He is faithful and righteous to forgive us our sins and to cleanse us from all unrighteousness.*" I have actually already covered this with respect to confessing sin. Please note, John does not say that we have to ask for forgiveness. In fact, Christians do not need to ask for forgiveness because it has already been applied. John is telling us that we need to confess our sin, which is completely different. Jesus taught people to pray the Lord's Prayer in which they were to ask forgiveness ("*forgive us our debts*"), but that was before the cross!

Confession of sin is in respect to our fellowship with God. When we sin, the Holy Spirit will let us know that we have done so, and this feeling of guilt (or grieving the Spirit) prompts us to recognize our sin. When we recognize it, we should immediately confess it. This is, in effect, fully agreeing with God that we have done something wrong. *"Yes, Lord, I agree completely with you. I have sinned and I'm confessing that to you right now. Thank you so much for your forgiveness and thank you that your Holy Spirit lives within me to keep me on the straight and narrow. I praise you Lord for your faithfulness, even when I am not faithful."*

There is a growing segment within Christendom that believes that when we sin, we should beat ourselves up. We should feel like scum. We should treat ourselves as the worms we are – yet is this Scriptural?

What about the Prodigal Son? He sinned terribly. He demanded his inheritance (while his father was still alive!), went out and partied like there was no tomorrow, then sunk to the lowest level possible by feeding pigs – not a good thing for a Jew.

Yet what happened to the young man? He came to his senses and realized that maybe his father might be willing to take him back if he went to him groveling and offered his services as a slave, not even a son. So that's what he did, and when he saw his father, it is interesting to note that his father ran to his son and embraced him.

The young man had his speech ready to go. He told his father he would come back as a slave, not a son. His father would have none of it. He gave him a robe, put a ring on his finger, sandals on his feet, and took the fattened calf and slaughtered it. Why? Because of the fact that the father had his son back! His son, who was once dead because of his actions, was now alive. The forgiveness that the father had extended to his son was always there! Please note that the father was constantly looking for the son to return, which meant that he was always ready to pick up the relationship again. When the son tried to show his father how repentant he was and was willing to grovel to be accepted, his father dismissed it! He had already forgiven the son. The son needed simply to return.

The son was prepared to come back and work his butt off for his father, and he was willing to be treated no better than a slave. The father would not allow it and treated his son as his son.

Notice the older son, though – and you can read about this in Luke 15:11-32 – who was hard at work in the field. He was annoyed that his brother had returned. After all, the younger son took off and he, the older son, continued working, slaving away for the father and never asking for anything. Unfortunately, the older son did not even know his father because he misunderstood the father's expectations. The older son believed he had to work for his father's affections and appreciation. Meanwhile, the father simply wanted to have a real relationship with both of his sons. While the younger son had learned the truth about his father, the older son never learned that truth and, in essence, was living as the slave that the younger son said he would be for the father.

I fully believe that God is extremely quick to apply His forgiveness to our life when we confess our sins to Him. He wants to be and remain in fellowship with us and does not like it when we are out of fellowship with Him. We should not take that lightly or use it as a reason to sin!

The reality for me seems to be that eternal security is just that: eternal. It also appears to be unconditional. There are no strings attached either to receive it or keep it.

It's funny, but I read where people liken the doctrine of eternal security to Roman Catholic indulgences. In reality, it's the other way around. Those who believe they are in danger of losing their salvation are the ones who are constantly having to "look over their shoulder" as it were, always having to maintain their salvation by their own works. If they do not continue to work to maintain their salvation, they are in danger of losing it. Isn't this what Roman Catholicism can be interpreted as teaching? Indulgences are merely another way of maintaining salvation that allow the penitent to spend less time in purgatory, which is, by the way, another form of "*payment*" to maintain salvation.

I doubt seriously that this article is the final word on the subject (and it shouldn't be). Not a chance. Hopefully, though, I have given you some food for thought. If you disagree with me, that's fine. Take it to the Lord in prayer. There is no point in arguing with me about it to try to convince yourself that you are right.

Thanks for reading, and I hope you will complete this book before you make any decisions. May the Lord bless you in your relationship with Him by opening your eyes to the tremendous riches we have in Jesus, riches that are beyond compare and will not be fully realized until we are with Him.

Chapter 2

Lordship Salvation: Right or Wrong?

"Wherefore if any man is in Christ, he is a new creature: the old things are passed away; behold, they are become new." – 2 Corinthians 5:17

I received a note from a friend about the topic of Lordship Salvation not long ago. He also commented on the article I referenced previously (in the last chapter) regarding the question of whether or not our future sins are automatically forgiven.

I responded to my friend who also said he *agreed* with the writer of the article when he stated that to teach that our future sins are forgiven is *blasphemy*. By that definition, then, I am a blasphemer.

I asked him his views on the article, he responded, and then I responded to him. I'm leaving names completely out of this because it serves no purpose. His comments below are italicized and mine are not.

I know that this issue has been written about repeatedly. I know that John MacArthur, for instance, has been accused of teaching Lordship Salvation, and I don't believe that is the case. I have his books and as I can see how people might misinterpret MacArthur's teachings on the subject, I fully believe that this is exactly what they have done. I believe MacArthur was emphasizing God's work of sanctification in the life of the believer. I also believe it is a good yardstick for us that if I can look back over my life and see no progress, no growing desire not to sin, and no greater desire to commune with God and become more like the character of Jesus, then maybe there is something wrong. That "maybe" is that there is a possibility I am not saved if my life appears to have grown no closer to God and no further from sin.

In reality, the issue of Lordship Salvation is a very difficult topic to explain. People on both sides of the aisle can use the same Scripture references in their attempt to prove their opposing points. The basic problem, though, seems to be found in the meaning of the word "repent." For some, this involves agonizing over my sin until the weight of it makes it impossible for me to stand, so I become broken. This should happen often in my life because of the tremendous evil that is sin, so naturally, if I do not understand this as being terribly evil and react to it with the proper feelings and emotion, then how could I possibly be living for God? How could I possibly understand just how evil sin is as God sees it? How could there be true repentance?

If I feel terrible about my sin – if I go through life with an attitude of constant repentance – then the belief is that I am closer (Lordship salvation proponents believe) to understanding just how bad sin is, and if I understand how terrible sin is, then I have proven to God that I am truly repentant for my sin. It may involve beating myself up emotionally (or going so far as beating myself up physically as Martin Luther of the Reformation did). But until I come to an abject awareness of just how terrible my sin is, then there has been no real repentance. As far as I can tell, this is the Lordship Salvation dogma at its core. To me, this is tragic, and I will have more to say on this subject in future posts. For now, let me post my friend's comments and my responses.

Oh, and by the way, I am *not* posting this topic to enter into debates. Debates are pointless. I know that if you believe in Lordship Salvation, I can't convince you of anything different. You should probably know also that your arguments will not likely convince me either. This is not to say that either of us are arrogant, but hopefully it means that we have *studied* the issue and arrived at a conclusion that we believe is based on Scriptures, yet open to any correction by the Spirit. If not, then we *are* arrogant.

So by posting this topic, I am not inviting debate. If you want to briefly share your opinion feel free. If you do so in attack mode, your comment will not be posted.

This is absolutely a very difficult issue to discuss because there is so much involved in it. For me, I believe when I receive the Lord, He becomes my Savior *and* my Lord at the same time. The Holy Spirit takes up residence within me, seals me, and activates His Presence within me, recreating the wonderful and perfect image of Jesus. This certainly doesn't mean I will never sin, but just as the athlete tries and fails but gets up, dusts him/herself off and moves on, Christians – I believe – should do the same thing. Far from minimizing or "cheapening" God's grace, it proves that we understand the nature of that grace and we are extremely grateful for it. I will try to develop this more over the next few posts. For now, here is the response I had for my friend, and again, his comments are mixed throughout in italics and are between the lines of asterisks.

****

Hi [friend],

"It is cheap grace. Where is the accountability if one does not have to repent for sins? Of course Christ died for all sins, but the opposite of what [the author of the article] is teaching is cheap grace or a license to sin."

Amazing how many people think this, [friend]. I believe I covered this quite well in the article I just wrote. Either you didn't read it or you read it through your Lordship Salvation glasses. You are unfortunately assuming that the Holy Spirit is completely *inactive* in the *authentic* Christian's life here.

I think the main sticking point is the definition of "*repent*." Some, like [the writer of the article] and people like [certain well-known evangelists] believe that if we do not have this constant fear of God's anger, then we are not really living the life that God wants us to live. Yes, I believe that there should always be a reverential fear of God. I do *not* believe that I need to beat myself up either emotionally or physically in order to somehow prove to God that I am really sorry for my sin(s).

"I can do as I please, my sins are forgiven."

Again, I covered this when I noted that **authentic** Christians do **not** want to sin. There are plenty of professing Christians who certainly live like this and it is what gives the Church a bad name. It also explains why there are so many people today who say that God is judging His Church. That's garbage. His actual *invisible* Church is doing just fine. It's the TARES within the VISIBLE Church that are wreaking havoc. They are the ones who are living like the devil.

"If one does not have to worry about sin then where is Christianity?"

So you think God wants us to focus on our *sins*? The idea that we must have this *lifestyle of repentance* is simply man's way of adding to God's salvation, a requirement that makes us feel that we are "doing something" to help in God's salvation. The reality is that God has freed us to a *life of love*. People like [the author of the article] don't seem to understand that this freedom creates within us the desire to *serve* God, not by focusing on sin, but by focusing on *God*, something the Law would not allow. When you are under the Law, you focus on how many times you break that Law and how terrible you feel because of it. When you are under Grace, you realize just how precious you are to God and how much He loves you. It is *that* understanding that keeps us from *wanting* to follow the dictates of sin.

"[the author of the article] is correct and what many are calling legalism is called sanctification in scripture. Once saved our responsibility to live a holy and acceptable life is foremost."

Actually, *in your opinion*, [the author of the article] is correct. In my opinion he is dead wrong. Sanctification is a process that is fully *directed* by the Holy Spirit. You think we can resist the Holy Spirit? Temporarily maybe, but not for long. If I am sealed by the Holy Spirit, I become *His*, lock, stock, and barrel. Because of this, He takes the lead and is fully in charge of my life.

"Christ said, if you love me obey my commandments. "

Yeah, okay, so why are you focusing on your sin?

"We are bound to responsibility once we accept Christ as our savior. Paul in Romans 12:1 calls it 'our reasonable service.' To do opposite and to think opposite is cheap grace."

Again, you are assuming that if I sin, I don't care about it. You are also assuming that repentance means I have to feel as though I am a worthless pig. If I do not come to that point, then there has been no real repentance and if there is no real repentance, then God will not apply His forgiveness. By the way, I don't "*accept*" Christ as Savior. I *receive* salvation because He opened my eyes to the truth and allowed me to embrace it. I'm not referring to prevenient grace here. I'm simply stating that *unless* God works in the life of the individual, no one would ever choose to "*accept*" Jesus.

Martin Luther lived like this and he was miserable. There was no fruit of the Spirit as we read in 1 Corinthians 13. Because of it, he wound up hating the Jews and became extremely anti-Semitic.

Unfortunately, I believe what [the author of the article] is teaching (aside from calling me a *blasphemer*) is that there is actual work that I need to do, heavy, back-breaking work that will constantly threaten to overwhelm me as a Christian. Yet, Jesus Himself said that we should take His burden on ourselves, because it is *light* and *easy to bear*. Not according to [the author of the article] or [certain well-known evangelist], or others like that who believe that the life of a Christian is much more difficult than what Jesus says. Apparently, they know better than He does.

We could unfortunately go back and forth quoting Scripture to each other until the cows come home and neither of us would be convinced. The reality for me is that I do not believe Lordship Salvation is Scriptural.

I am saved. I have received salvation from the Lord, which is an ongoing result of my faith in Him and will culminate in the next life. He is also my Lord because that is the position He is in over me. Either I submit my life to Him voluntarily, or He will force me to do it through loving chastisement. There is no "if I make Him Lord" about it.

People are attracted to Lordship Salvation because it gives them something to *do*, something to *work for*, something to *achieve*. Instead of glorying in His love for us, and being thankful for all that He has done and will do in and through us, the focus for the Lordship Salvation person is solely on SELF, yet it is so insidious that most people are not even aware of it at all. It is how – I believe – Satan traps believers into participating in a form of "indulgences" because they think they have to somehow "pay" for their own sin by feeling terrible about it and agonizing over it. If they do not do that, then their salvation comes into question.

Many people who believe in Lordship Salvation also often believe that salvation can be *lost*. These folks do not believe in *unconditional* eternal security and in essence – whether they agree or disagree – they wind up believing in *conditional* salvation and there is nothing eternal about that. I've talked to people who have told me that you cannot know you are saved until you actually stand before the Lord. Really? Interesting.

While I can understand people wanting to be holy (sanctified, or set apart), the disagreement comes in with what that really *means*. We both probably know that Sanctification is really two-pronged. There is something that God does FOR us – *Positional Sanctification*, and there is something that I, as a Christian ***participate*** in – *Progressive Sanctification*. This progressive sanctification is where I *walk in the newness of the Spirit*, instead of the death of the old man, yet it is only done with the strength and empowering of the Holy Spirit.

2 Corinthians 5:17 states, "Wherefore if any man is in Christ, he is a new creature: the old things are passed away; behold, they are become new."

I am no longer the old Fred. I'm completely new. This new nature has already been given to the believer, but its transforming power is experienced when a Christian becomes sanctified to follow after the things of God. How do I do that? I *mainly* do this by studying His Word and allowing His Word to transform me into the image and character of Jesus and through prayer. He creates within me the desire to *ignore* SELF (the flesh). He creates within me the desire to follow Him and submit to Him. I believe Lordship Salvation creates the desire to – unfortunately – *cater* to SELF without realizing it.

When I sin, I recognize it and admit it as quickly as possible, not with a laissez-faire attitude, but with an understanding that what I did was wrong and God wants me to quickly recognize it and confess it so that I can return to the fellowship I had with Him before I sinned.

When I do something wrong against my wife, she does NOT expect me to beat myself up. She is ready and *quick* to forgive me. I don't have to go to her on my knees begging for her forgiveness. I come to her and apologize for my behavior. If *she* is that quick to forgive, how much more is God toward His children? Would you call what my wife does "cheap grace"? If you did, you would be wrong. It is *because* of how quickly she forgives that I do not want to "sin" against her again. Unfortunately, I know that I will likely sin against her again and she with me.

Certain individuals believe that considerable time should be spent conjuring up emotional turmoil so that we can somehow "prove" to God that we are really, *really* sorry for what we did.

This was *not* the attitude of the Prodigal Son's father. Even as his son *tried* to give the speech he had prepared, saying how bad he was and how he merely wanted to be a slave in his father's employ, the father would have none of it.

It is too bad that this "holiness" movement has risen to the level it has risen to because in my view, it simply adds requirements to salvation that do not exist. Many who believe in Lordship Salvation also believe in a form of Dominism – the idea is that as more

Christians become involved politically, they will gain more control over their area of influence and that area – whether a city or a nation – will become governed by Christian principles. Sounds like what you said to me the other day. Call it Dominism, Christian Reconstructionism, or whatever you'd like, but the meaning is the same. That's not what the Bible teaches, as far as I can tell.

My job as a Christian is to fully *cooperate* with God, not beat myself up, not go through life believing that if I do not castigate myself for every sin I commit, I'm worthless and have not confessed it properly. My job is to believe that God in Christ is the Author *and Perfector* of my salvation. Yes, I work *with* Him, but he carries the bulk of it so that I will become like Him. I can't do that, no matter how terrible I make myself feel and it does not impress God either.

Or, I guess I could do what certain people teach and take on the attitude that Martin Luther adopted. Hey, I could even start whipping myself to make me feel better!

Sorry [friend], Lordship Salvation is merely another name someone has given to make the concept of "indulgences" sound Christian. It adds nothing to His salvation, but pretends that it does. In the process, it leaves people feeling worthless and ashamed. You think that's the way God wants us to go through life? Sorry, but I do not recall Paul mentioning this in 1 Corinthians 13…

If we are to feel like crap for our sin, then that is all we will ever be able to do in this life because of all our sin. The focus is SELF.

You know, I've been called a heretic for my views on the PreTrib Rapture. I've been told I will likely lose my salvation because of it. I've been called a blasphemer because I do not believe in Lordship Salvation. The way Christians toss around these terms is a bit much.

****

Because this is such an important issue, I chose to write this book. Again, will I convince anyone of anything? It is not likely, though I'm hoping that for those who have not made a decision, they will certainly prayerfully consider what I have to say.

There was a time in my life when all I did was focus on how bad I was, how sinful I am, and how unworthy I was/am to receive salvation. Certainly, this is true, but believing that this attitude needs to be an integral part of the Christian's daily walk is foolhardy and anti-Christian, in my opinion.

What child would love his/her father if that father expected them to denigrate themselves every time they made a mistake? I have a daughter and a son. They are both adults now, but I remember a period of time when I was constantly on my son's case. He couldn't do many things right, as far as I was concerned. Thankfully, the Lord helped me realize that while loving discipline is certainly necessary, ultimately, it is love, not discipline, that wins out.

I could take the time to *still* correct my son about this or that and sometimes, depending upon the situation, I still do, but one thing I do *not* do is try to make him feel as though when he messes up he should feel worthless! There is no point to that because it simply *discourages* him and gives him a reason to be angry. Both Ephesians 6:4 and Colossians 3:21 speak of not provoking or embittering our children. Paul is telling us to *not* make your children feel worthless by constantly pointing out all the wrong things they do.

Yet certain teachers believe that we have an obligation as Christians to make ourselves feel *embittered* when we sin! How ludicrous, and the belief that if I do not take the time to castigate myself when I sin I am somehow cheapening grace is also ludicrous. God poured out His wrath on Jesus as He hung on the cross, yet many believe that we are supposed to pour out our wrath on ourselves in repentance every time we sin and if we don't, we are taking sin too lightly, cheapening God's grace. This is so wrong in my opinion.

Isn't it funny how much we focus on our wrongs, instead of what God is making us *into*? This is not say that I should ignore my sin, but like Paul says, I should cast off every work of darkness. Can you picture this? It is throwing those things aside and walking away from them. Our attitude needs to be that of a warrior in battle, but always with our eyes on Jesus. The warrior focuses on the goal, not getting sidetracked by missteps (or sin, in our case). Can you imagine a warrior belittling himself, castigating himself, and literally hating himself every time he did something wrong in battle? He wouldn't last long at all.

Satan is our accuser. He works with our flesh to mount the effort to destroy or weaken us. If he can get us to focus on how bad we are (which is not true if we are IN Christ, meaning if we have salvation), he can successfully get us to take our eyes off Christ and put them onto ourselves. That's the *last* place our eyes should be. They should be completely and forever *glued* to Jesus, the Author and Finisher of our faith! Try looking at Jesus AND yourself at the same time. I triple dog dare ya! You can't do it.

If Satan wants to accuse you of sin, *agree with him*, confess it to the Lord and *move* on. If Jesus is not condemning you, how do you justify condemning yourself? Jesus goes to bat for you as your Advocate *against* Satan. Yet too many people are not only agreeing with Satan about our sin (that's fine), but also agreeing with everything he says about us! He's a liar and a murderer. I am saved by grace! I am a new creature. All things are past and everything is new. I walk in the newness of Life through the indwelling power of the Holy Spirit.

When God looks at me, He sees Christ's righteousness. For those who take sin so lightly that it makes no impact on their lives, I contend that they do not know Jesus in the first place, because He will *not allow that attitude to continue* in one of His own.

Chapter 3

Claiming vs. Being

"...ungodly persons who turn the grace of our God into licentiousness and deny our only Master and Lord, Jesus Christ." Jude 1:4

Those people who claim the title of Christian and live like they aren't cannot be Christians in my view. I frankly do not see how it is possible.

For instance, it was reported that two women were married recently - one a "Christian" and the other a Jew. Do I think for a moment that the one who says she is a Christian *is*, in fact, a Christian? No, because as Paul says, we know them by their fruit. She is Christian in name only, just as the Jewish woman is Jewish by ethnicity only.

I think many under the heading of Lordship Salvation seem not to differentiate between people who *say* they are Christians and those who truly *are* Christians. Maybe some do, but in general, it seems that those folks do not.

If a person *is* a Christian and they still sin (occasionally, not as a lifestyle) - even *wanting* to sin at times - this does *not* mean that Jesus is no longer that person's Lord. It means they screwed up and they need to change their direction in a hurry or God will do it for them.

I fully believe that when I received salvation from Jesus He also became my Lord, and that will never change. When I sin, He is *still* Lord, but for the moment, I *acted* like He was not my Lord. It did not change the truth, though. The Holy Spirit within me directs me to walk in His ways and please Him. Because of the sin nature we will still sin and sometimes we will *want* to sin, or more accurately, our sin nature will make us *feel* as though we want to sin. We can either agree and succumb or ignore it in His strength. If I sin, for that moment I have followed my own desires, but it is easy to get back to the right place by recognizing it and turning from it.

I cannot separate my salvation from His being Lord. In my mind, it is the same thing with these two areas completely intertwined; however, there are degrees of maturity in many Christians and it takes time for people to grow in their relationship with Him.

When I was a kid, there were times when I acted out and I did things that were wrong. This did not mean that my parents stopped being my parents or had no authority over me. It means I simply decided to go against what they wanted me to do. They *remained* my parents and got me back on the correct path. Why? It was because they had that authority. They *were* my parents.

The main problem I see with Lordship advocates is that they *seem* to emphasize *guilt* as the motivating factor, and yes, we are guilty. I'm talking about trying to make people feel guilty about their lives on an ongoing basis. It is a difficult road to hoe though. *Grace* emphasizes *love* as the motivating factor. I submit myself to the Lord because He loved/loves me and gave Himself for me. The more I grow in that love, the more I want to make sure that my life is dedicated to serving Him.

For the person who is not actually saved but *thinks* they are, maybe they do need to feel the guilt, because they obviously have a terrible understanding of God's grace and Christianity in general. True grace does not give a person a license to sin, no more than my wife's love toward me creates in me the desire to cheat on her. Her love and grace causes me to return that in kind.

If I said I was her husband and lived as though I was not, then I have obviously completely misunderstood the meaning of being a husband. It's not *grace* or love that I have misconstrued. It's the meaning of "*husband*" that I have misunderstood. It's the same with those who say they are Christians but live as though they are not. It is not grace that they have misunderstood. It is the meaning of authentic Christianity that they have misunderstood.

Some evangelists need to make it clear that they are talking mainly to non-Christians, or people who *say* they are Christians but likely aren't. They should treat people as though they are *not* saved instead of heaping on the guilt to make them realize how rotten they are. The problem is that much of what many "Lordship salvation" evangelists say uses guilt cues to prompt people to act. I really do not see that in Scripture. Guilt has no staying power. Yes, the apostle Paul points some of these things out, but his overall message is not focusing on "*guilting*" people into the Kingdom. In Galatians, he was extremely upset because of the Judaizers and what they were trying to accomplish. He was angry with those in the church for listening to them. He emphasized, though, God's *grace* over against the Law.

Guilt - in my view - is a very poor taskmaster as far as keeping a person from sinning. While it might force us into acting a certain way outwardly, it does *nothing* to create a loving relationship with God from within. Only grace does that, in my view, and I think this is where many Lordship Salvation advocates fall down. They are very good at emphasizing His Lordship and using a tremendous amount of guilt and negativity to accomplish it. They are very poor at focusing on God's grace because they think if they focus on grace too much (how much is too much?) they will foster the wrong idea of what salvation means and what it means to have Him as Lord.

I do agree that His Lordship over all aspects of my life *is* inherent within salvation. I also believe that it is a growing thing for all true Christians that only *begins* when we receive Jesus.

There is an interesting story to tell that highlights this point (and I've paraphrased it here). Alexander the Great was one of the greatest warriors of all time, gaining a larger empire than Rome in a very short time. Apparently, during one particular battle, one of his soldiers got cold feet and stayed hidden from the fighting. He was caught by the others and brought before Alexander.

As the soldier stood trembling, Alexander asked him what his name was. The soldier very meekly replied "*Alexander.*" Alexander the Great couldn't believe what he'd just heard and asked him again to hear the same reply. You could hear a pin drop in the room. Alexander the Great was incensed and everyone thought he would give the order to have the man killed.

Instead, with great anger, yet contained, he looked at the man and said: "*Either change your **name**, or change your **ways**!*"

Chapter 4

The Prodigal Son

"A man had two sons. The younger of them said to his father, 'Father, give me the share of the estate that falls to me.'" Luke 15:11

E ven though we have already touched on the issue of the Prodigal Son, I think it's worthy enough to consider in far more depth. The Prodigal Son – for me – is a story of a loving father and two sons. Initially both sons seem to actually hate their father.

This hatred on the part of the two sons stems from one thing: *they simply did not know their father at all*. Both sons saw their father as a cruel taskmaster, someone who really cared little for their welfare and was all about getting the job done no matter what it took.

Because of this terribly erroneous attitude, both sons viewed their father as something he was not. This is important to understand because it lays the framework for the entire parable. Both sons viewed their father as mean, tyrannical, obsessed with work, unloving, and completely aloof to them and their needs.

I used to be a bit confused by this parable. Was the Prodigal Son an object lesson in a person *coming to know the Lord in salvation?* Was the story about a young man who "falls away" then "returns"? I didn't know what to make of it. Let's take a look at the story and break it down.

One thing is crucial to understand before we get into this parable. We need to understand that in the beginning of the story, neither son displayed any type of love for their father. While the older son was *loyal*, even there his loyalty was not born of love, but of duty. The older son felt compelled to slave away for the father, and he felt this way because he never gained a sense that his father loved him.

The younger son felt the same way, yet he was much more of an outward rebel. He wanted to do things his way, and he was strong enough in his own personality to go off on his own.

If we turn to Luke 15:11-32, we come to the parable of the Prodigal Son. In this particular chapter, Jesus is teaching the crowds the definition of God's love. He first speaks of the lost sheep, noting that there is not one shepherd in the audience who would ignore the fact that one of his sheep was gone. Oh, and by the way, it is important to note that this entire chapter is predicated upon the charge that Jesus ate with "sinners" (cf. Luke 15:1-2). This claim by the Pharisees and religious leaders was certainly true. Jesus *did* eat with and even welcome the average person – sinners by God's definition – to Him because that is what He came to do. Jesus did not need to justify Himself to those religious leaders, but what He did instead was present a number of parables to point out how wrong they were about people.

Not only did Jesus publicly declare they were wrong, but He did so in a way that was characteristic of how He handled such charges. Beyond this, the folks listening to Him would understand exactly what God the Father's love was like for them.

You see, the average person of Jesus' day was taught to believe that they were *worthless*. They were scum, looked down upon by those in authority and made to feel as though they simply never measured up.

In truth, we do *not* measure up as far as God is concerned, which is why Jesus came, lived among us without sin, died a criminal's painful death, and shed His blood for you and me. His life and death fulfilled the Law and allowed Him to be the sacrifice for our sin. Because of His perfection, the grave could not hold Him and He rose three days later.

What the religious leaders of Jesus' day did not understand was that they were no better off than the average person. Unfortunately, those same religious leaders believed that they were fully accepted by God, and they took pride in that false notion.

Jesus tried to dispel those arrogant beliefs in the religious leaders but for the most part was unsuccessful. This lack of success was due solely to the fact that the religious leaders wanted no part of Jesus and what He taught.

The average person, though, wanted what Jesus offered. When He was charged with receiving sinners, He readily acknowledged that this is exactly what He did and then proceeded to emphasize that by teaching the crowds with three parables.

He first speaks of the lost sheep. No shepherd worth his salt would ever allow a sheep to go unaccounted for, unless that shepherd was simply a hired hand and had no investment in those sheep, either financially or emotionally.

A good shepherd would do whatever was necessary to ensure the safety of his sheep. If he had 100 sheep, and one wandered off, he would leave the 99 to go off and search for the missing one. All in the crowd – even the religious leaders – could appreciate that fact. Please notice also that Jesus speaks specifically of the one who "repents" in this brief parable.

Next Jesus speaks of the woman and the missing coin (cf. Luke 15:8-10). If the woman has ten silver coins and then realizes that one of them is missing, she will essentially look under every piece of furniture and in every corner of her home to find that missing piece of silver. When she finally discovers it, she will rejoice and share the news with her neighbors.

After these brief introductory parables, Jesus digs deeper and shares a longer story with the crowd. This story is very interesting because as the first two parables – the parable of the lost sheep and the parable of the lost coin – lay the foundation, the parable of the prodigal son goes much further and deeper with the message. It outlines just exactly how God the Father sees us because of the work that Jesus did on our behalf.

The prodigal son's father in the story is very loving. One wonders how these two sons could have missed that, but when we see how often Jesus was misunderstood by the religious leaders of His day, the answer becomes rather obvious. They missed it because they were blind. They did not want to see their father in any other way except the way they had conjured him up in their minds.

To the sons, the father was a tyrant. He was constantly expecting them to work and slave away because of the fact that they were his sons. In the minds of the two sons, their father saw them as little better than slaves. He obviously worked them as slaves and expected a great deal from them. But is that the way the father was in the story? Let's find out.

Luke 15:11-13

"A man had two sons. The younger of them said to his father, 'Father, give me the share of the estate that falls to me.' So he divided his wealth between them. And not many days later, the younger son gathered everything together and went on a journey into a distant country, and there he squandered his estate with loose living."

In the verses above, we are introduced to the situation that Jesus presents to the gathered crowd. Notice the son – the *younger* son at that! – goes to his father and essentially demands from his father the inheritance he would normally only receive *after* his father had died! Talk about temerity! I cannot imagine my son coming to me and saying, "*Dad, I know you're not dead yet, but I really want you to give me what I would inherit from you after you die.*"

But the most fascinating part of this is not that the son asks for his inheritance while his father is still alive, but that the father does what his son asks. Why would a father do this? If my son asked me, I'd tell him in no uncertain terms that he was asking for the wrong thing and showing disrespect for me as his father. My son would not ask me, though.

So why did the son in the family in Jesus' parable believe it was fine to make this request of his father? We're not sure, and we could easily try to use the latest psychology to try and determine the answer, but I think the simplest reason is because Jesus put this parable together to ultimately show how loving the father was to his sons, though they obviously could not or would not appreciate it. It is also possible that both of these young men viewed their father as something different from what he was to them. How often have we read of young people treating their parents with disdain because they either did not really know their parents or due to some other reason?

In this particular case, it appears as though the father was wealthy, as mentioned in verse 12 where we read that the father "*divided his wealth between them.*" We also learn as the story unfolds that the older son at least worked hard, so he did not appear to be spoiled, though we understand that the younger son may not have been such a hard worker. Then again, maybe he was a hard worker and just got tired of it. In his young, immature mind, he had worked long and hard enough and wanted to enjoy life now before he got old. Maybe this prompted him to make a request of this nature.

For whatever reason, the young son sets propriety aside and decides that it is reasonable to expect his father to give him his inheritance now. The father gives his son what he asks for, and he appears to do it without quibbling or arguing. He simply does it.

No sooner does the young man receive his inheritance than he is off on a journey of a lifetime! He heads off into the sun for a better life of fun and adventure, and before you know it, he is spending his part of the inheritance on fast living. Jesus points out that soon enough, all of his money has been squandered away with nothing to show for it.

The young son did not take the time to even think about investing it so that he would receive a return on his investment, which would allow him to continue his life of comfort. Instead, the young son lived for the moment, spending his money on whatever suited his pleasure.

Certainly, people are attracted to people who have money. They like to hang around because it makes them feel as though they themselves are rich as well. Beyond this, there is definitely a good chance that if they become part of that rich person's inner circle, they will directly benefit from that person's wealth.

These types of individuals are merely leeches, preying on the unwary by becoming a sycophant. They are the "yes" people who, in this case, tell the young man what he wants to hear. They ingratiate themselves to him, making him think that they are friends to him because of who he is, not because of the money he has in his possession. Of course, proof of their real motives is in the fact that as soon as the money is gone, so are they, off to find another individual they can charm so that that new person will supply their need.

The young man – we are told – squandered his estate with loose living. The sense here, of course, is *immorality*. He did whatever he wanted to do and he did it because he could and because there was no one to tell him to avoid such behavior. If he lived at home, there is an excellent chance that his father would try to redirect his thoughts and actions away from such living, but now that he was on his own, he could do whatever he wanted to do and it did not matter. There was no one to tell him that he was heading off down the wrong trail.

This could very well be why the young man felt the need to leave, and he knew that he could not simply leave without visible means of support, so he entreated his father to give him what was coming to him now as opposed to later. The father likely figured that rather than try to *tell* his son what would happen, he would simply let him go to figure it out for himself. If he could be taught this lesson on his own, the father might gain his son.

Luke 15:14-15
"Now when he had spent everything, a severe famine occurred in that country, and he began to be impoverished. So he went and hired himself out to one of the citizens of that country, and he sent him into his fields to feed swine."

So the results of living on his own, doing whatever he wanted to do, not having a plan for income, and involving himself in acts of immorality with others who likely encouraged that lifestyle became all too obvious. The young son woke up one morning to the realization that he was out of money. He had no way to support himself at all.

The young son had enjoyed his living – for however long it had lasted – and since he was living from day to day, he had made no plans at all for the future, likely thinking it would not come. He certainly had not counted on the fact that he would run out of money, and if he did think of it, figured he would cross that bridge when he came to it.

Well, that day came and he crossed that bridge. With no money, no friends, no way to support himself, and a severe famine occurring, he had no choice but to actually *work* for something again. Wait a minute, isn't this why he had left his father's estate in the first place? He obviously did not like working and felt he had worked hard enough. Now it was time to party, so bring it on!

Reality smacked him right across the face and he was met with the realization that without work, he would have no food, so he took a job tending pigs. The irony here is that as a young Jewish man, his father would not have owned pigs because as animals with cloven hooves, they were considered unclean. They would not have been part of his father's herds of farm animals.

If you have never been around pigs, you should know that the stench from a pig pen is palpable. It is *bad*. The smell of dirty pigs is bad enough, but add to that the picture of these same pigs relieving themselves in their pig pens, walking and rolling in it, and you get a sense of how bad that smell becomes.

Cows can smell much better, and even their manure – because of the fact they eat mainly hay and oats – gives them and their excrement a much nicer, even healthy smell, at least compared to pigs.

The only thing I have smelled that is worse than pig excrement is chicken dung! I recall living in upstate New York where there were many cattle farms and farms with chickens. It was fun to take a drive in the country and just follow the road to see where it would lead.

At times, the land was so beautiful that you might park your car and walk for a ways just to enjoy the beauty of the land and the fresh smell in the air of alfalfa or hay. It was really nice.

However, depending upon where you drove, you also might run across a farm field with a strange, very large whitish pile at one end of that field. As you drew closer to it, the smell of chicken manure would hit your nose, making you speed your car up to pass it quickly. Pigs and chickens have nasty smells all their own.

Yet this young Jewish man found himself working among the pigs. The irony is hard to miss. Because of the severe famine, who really knows how many jobs were available. I doubt that the young man would have taken this one if something else had been there for him, but this seems to have been what was there and he needed a job, so he took it.

I can't imagine working with pigs. Growing up in NY, a number of my friends had dairy farms and so I would visit them every once in a while. I would help them feed the cows and the calves and do their chores. Not once did I ever have to feed pigs or chickens because they generally did not have these animals on their dairy farms. Some had a few chickens to provide fresh eggs for the family, but most of the animals were cows. It was sometimes messy work, but enjoyable, if you didn't mind getting a bit dirty.

But this young man not only got dirty, but terribly stinky. It shows just how far he went, from leaving the comfort of home to the reality of life without a way to support himself. Such is life, but of course, in this case, it could have been avoided altogether had the son had a more realistic view of life in the first place. As we'll see, this turned out to be a very good life lesson for the son.

Luke 15:16

"And he would have gladly filled his stomach with the pods that the swine were eating, and no one was giving anything to him."

Here we see the predicament of having no money to buy food and being hungry. What do you do? It had gotten so bad for the young man that he would have stooped to eating the same food that the pigs were eating, but no one was giving him anything.

At least he didn't scrounge in the dirt and muck to grab some of the food that had been given to the pigs. Nonetheless, he was hungry. What could he do?

As often happens, God waits until we have exhausted all of our means of trying to do for ourselves. He knows when we get to our lowest point, the only thing we can do is look up.

Initially, the son had a decent life, living with his father and having his needs met. Apparently, that wasn't good enough; he had come to see living under his father's authority as a noose around his neck, and it had started to chafe him big time. He wanted out, so he decided to disrespect his father tremendously by insisting that his father give him his inheritance now.

The father complied, though he could have used the situation to disown his son for abject disrespect. Once the son received his inheritance, he was gone, off to carve out his own life under his own authority.

We see how that turned out for him. At first, everything was fine as he spent money like water from a faucet. This was the good life, the life he was obviously meant to live.

It is clear that not once did the young man realize that had not his father worked hard for what he had, the son would have had little to support his lifestyle. That didn't matter because the son was finally free of his father's autocratic rule. The son was now his own man.

He was also very immature and, some might say, stupid, because while he had money, he also had friends. He never made the connection until the money was gone along with those he thought were friends.

Now the son was at the bottom of the barrel, feeding pigs and yearning for some of the food they ate. What to do?

Luke 15:17
"But when he came to his senses, he said, 'How many of my father's hired men have more than enough bread, but I am dying here with hunger!'"

I appreciate the language here. Jesus says the young man "came to his senses." Most of us have been in situations like this, but maybe not quite as bad. Nonetheless, there comes a time when the light bulb clicks on in our head. We realize that there actually is another way out, as opposed to – in this young man's case – starving to death.

Of course, in almost all cases, this way out involves being humbled. There is no other way. It is at this point that people have two choices. They can give in and humble themselves, or they can continue to fight against it, maintaining their pride in the situation.

Fortunately for this young man, he proved he had some sense. He realized that his father's servants had plenty to eat and food was not something they worried about at all. Because their stomachs were always full, they were able to concentrate on other things.

The young man was now at the point of always thinking of food. He was always hungry, and he finally woke to the realization that he did not have to live that way.

This is the point at which the Lord can begin to break through to a person. Because he loves us so much, He will often place us in a corner where we can come to the realization that life does not have to be the way it is, and if we are willing to humble ourselves so that we will see the truth, we can then *embrace* that truth and go from there.

It is sad that many resolutely refuse to see the truth, even at that point. If they do begin to see the truth, there is still the chance that they will reject it.

The young man *could* have said that he would not go back to his father no matter what. He could have put his foot down and rejected the dictates of truth, never embracing it.

People do this all the time. We work ourselves into corners and then become angry with God or someone else instead of recognizing and accepting the responsibility for our actions.

God is not holding it over our heads so that we will wallow in guilt. He does not want to break us in that way. He wants only to help us get past the pride we may feel so that we are free to see and embrace the truth of the situation.

The young man was truly coming to his senses. He was beginning to see the light. He understood that there was indeed another way out, rather than slowly starving to death. He saw the other road. Would he take it or proudly remain on his chosen path?

Do you see yourself in this situation at all? Maybe you have never been in the exact situation as the young man in the parable, but if you're human, there have likely been times when you proudly asserted yourself, believing that your way was the right way. You eventually came to a point where you were forced to conclude that things did not work out as you had expected them to work out. At that point, what was your response to the situation?

Luke 15:18-19

"I will get up and go to my father, and will say to him, 'Father, I have sinned against heaven, and in your sight; I am no longer worthy to be called your son; make me as one of your hired men'."

With this attitude seen in the above two verses, we see that the young man actually *won*. He saw the truth and embraced it. He did not shrink from it, hiding behind his pride. He understood what he must do to live and thrive, and he was absolutely willing to do that.

The Lord continually holds out his arms to the lost and rebellious of this world. He wants us to see His truth – the only truth – and after seeing it, He wants us to embrace it. Those who embrace it begin to be truly freed from the dictates of SELF. Those who might see and reject the truth remain beholden to SELF and, if they remain on that path, will ultimately die in their sin.

Even for Christians, pride can exert itself so that we close ourselves off from God. We can give into our pride and our rebellious nature due to the inherent sin nature that still exists within us.

The young man could have seen this truth and rejected it, digging in his heels. He could have said to himself how stupid it would be to go back to his father with his tail between his legs. His father would know that he (the young son) had failed. He wasn't going to give his father the pleasure of holding that over him. That's what he could have done, but fortunately for the young man, he did not go that route.

This is so beautiful the way this happened. First, the father allows his young son to go off on his own. He realizes that if he tried to stop him, it would not work at all and would likely backfire. So the father does what he know will cause him emotional pain and lets go of his son so that his son will hopefully learn a valuable lesson about life and the love of his father.

This is what God does for us. He allows us the room to fail because He knows that out of failure comes success. By success, I mean that people often embrace Him at the start if they are not Christians, or they will embrace Him *more* if they are Christians.

Again, the first step in embracing the truth is *recognizing* the situation. This is what the son did. He came to the conclusion that he was extremely hungry and there was no food for him. This realization brought him to the next step. The next step involved understanding that all was not lost. He actually had a choice in the matter. Would he now *embrace* that choice or reject it?

I believe that this is what the writer of Hebrews means when he talks about tasting the Lord and seeing that He is good, but then rejecting Him. The exact wording of Hebrews 6:4-6 is, "*For in the case of those who have once been enlightened and have tasted of the heavenly gift and have been made partakers of the Holy Spirit, and have tasted the good word of God and the powers of the age to come, and then have fallen away, it is impossible to renew them again to repentance, since they again crucify to themselves the Son of God and put Him to open shame.*"

I believe the writer of Hebrews is speaking of those who have *seen* the truth and that truth has *affected* them spiritually. They have not fully *embraced* it, but it has literally washed over them like a fresh spring. They become enlightened to the reality of God and His presence. They *begin* to understand and comprehend who God is and what He has accomplished for them.

If these people do not *fully embrace* that truth, letting go of pride and rejecting arguments against that truth, they will not have that chance again.

This is *not* like the person who hears the truth about Jesus several times during the course of their life and simply rejects it out of hand.

These people have not yet seen the truth. They hear the words and deny the truth because it has made no impact on them. These people will be given as many chances as possible throughout their lifetime to actually *see* the truth so that they have the opportunity to *embrace* it.

It is the person who *clearly sees* the truth of the gospel that has the opportunity to *embrace* it. They are now at a crossroads in their life and they have the chance to receive that truth fully or reject it as being a lie.

In essence, then, this was where the young man was in the parable. He had gone his own way, done his own thing, and lived his own life without any consideration for his father. He fully enjoyed life and had enough money to allow him to live the way he wanted to live...for a time.

Once that money was gone, so were his so-called friends, as well as his lifestyle that he had craved. He could have become bitter. He actually could have become angry at his father for not trying to stop him from leaving. Why did his father just give into his demand? Why didn't his father reject the son's desire to have his inheritance now and leave?

The young son could have blamed the entire thing on his father, but he chose not to do that. It was because he chose not to entertain that blame that he was able to eventually see the truth of the situation. It was in seeing the truth that he was actually able to embrace it because he had knocked down any roadblocks that his pride might have placed up.

Had the young man blamed his father, his pride would have won. He would not have seen the truth of the situation, that he (the son) was responsible for his current predicament. He would not have come face to face with himself and the lie that he had been living.

It was at this juncture that he *began* to see the true nature of his father's love. He began to understand that it was *because* his father loved him that he allowed the son to walk away, taking with him his part of the inheritance which he had not deserved.

In other words, the son, instead of playing the blame game, literally did come to his senses and accepted responsibility for his situation. This was a sign of maturity. Because of this, the next bit of truth dawned on him.

The text tells us that *after* he realized that his father's servants ate until they were full, he crafted a plan that would bring him back to his father's house where he also would be able to eat until he was full. Notice the attitude of the young man now.

At first, he was arrogant, having been given so much in his life that he never truly appreciated it. His haughtiness caused him to think of himself more highly than he should have, and that caused him to choose a course that ultimately meant abject failure. Of course, he didn't see that coming because his eyes were only on himself.

Once he saw the truth of his situation and *accepted* it, he was then free to see the next step, which was the course of action he would take to right the terrible situation he had made for himself. He came to a point of realizing that since he no longer deserved to be called his father's son, he would confess that very fact to his father.

The son realized just how badly he had treated his father and how he had "sinned against heaven." Because of this realization, he believed that as a form of payment or penance he should be treated no better than one of his father's slaves.

Do you see the progression here? First, the son is resolutely proud and arrogant. Second, he lives the life that his pride pushed him to live. Third, when he comes to the end of that lifestyle, he winds up doing the very thing that would have brought dishonor to him and his family (which is why he admitted to himself that he had sinned against heaven and in the full view of his father). That sin started when he demanded of his father something he had no right to demand, his inheritance.

Fourth, the son finally begins to come to his senses. The truth begins to dawn on him. His pride was being defeated because of the truth. Notice again that though he could have hardened his heart against the truth, he chose not to do so. He allowed the truth to permeate his mind, and it did.

Fifth, once he contemplated the truth of the situation, he saw the only plausible choice that made sense to him. He believed that he should go back to his father and confess his sin to him. Moreover, he believed he should be willing to take on the job of a servant, no longer worthy of being called a son.

Some might look at this as abject sorrow or self-hatred and loathing. I don't see this at all. In fact, I see a son who had arrived at a conclusion which made him fully *free* and actually gave him *joy* in this situation. He had realized how stupid and selfish he had been and decided on a course of action to correct that problem he had created. That gave him an optimistic view of how his father would treat him.

We will see shortly that though the son believed his penance would be fulfilled by submitting to his father as a slave, his father had other ideas. This is extremely important to realize.

Luke 15:20
"So he got up and came to his father. But while he was still a long way off, his father saw him and felt compassion for him, and ran and embraced him and kissed him."

Please do not miss the important point made in the above text. The son got up and went to his father. That was important. In actuality, the son repented by understanding that his actions had been wrong, and he ultimately turned from those actions. That is the meaning of repentance, to turn away from that which is wrong, to go the other way. The son did this, but let's not ignore his father's reaction.

"While he was still a long way off, his father saw him and felt compassion for him…" Do you get the impression that the father had been in the habit of scanning the horizon on a daily basis? Does it appear to you that every day, he would look up and search as far as his eyes could see for any sign of a returning son?

I don't think it was accident or coincidence that allowed the father to see his son coming to him. I believe he deliberately chose to look for any sign that today might be the day when his wayward son would come home. Each morning, he started the day with, "will my son come home today?"

Today was that day! Today, as he scanned the horizon for any sign, he saw him! Yes, that was him! His beloved son, returning home! He was returning!

Now here is where it gets really interesting. The father *ran* to his son and embraced him. Wow, how could he do that? More importantly, we must understand that particular culture and how this act would have looked.

In those days, had the son done what he did, he would have been considered "dead" to his father. The father's friends and neighbors would have sided with the father and consoled him in his loss. For the sake of the father, they would not have talked about the son any longer. They would have acted as if that son had never been born because of the total disrespect that he had shown his father by doing what he had done.

Now, after however many weeks or months, the son was returning, and it is likely that the father was not the only one who saw him heading his way. Others may have seen him coming back, and they would have been prepared to ignore the son as if he did not exist because of how he had so badly mistreated his father.

Then something remarkable and completely unexpected happened. While the people watched the son return and expected the father to ignore him, he was actually *looking* at his son, watching him as he made the trip home! Why was he doing that? How could the father, who had been so ill-treated by his son, even *notice* his son?

But then something even more astonishing took place that the others never expected to see. The father was actually *running* to his son! How could he do this?

In those days, men wore robes that often went to a length just above the foot. When we read in Scripture the phrase "gird up your loins," what this is referring to is taking the folds of your robe and tucking them into your belt so that they would not get in your way when you worked or ran. Peasants and servants would do this, but never would a wealthy landowner do this because it was simply not something they did. They would never hurry to get someplace. They would never be in a situation where they would have to "show their legs" by tucking their robe into their belt.

Yet here was the father, either having tucked his robe into his belt or simply holding up the long folds of cloth so that he would not trip, running to meet his son! How could he do this?

Love. The father did this because he loved his son. The father knew that the son was returning not in willful pride but because he had seen the truth and turned away from his prideful living. The father knew that his son was coming home a different person, a wiser person, a more mature son. The son now understood what it meant to be a true son.

Not only does the father run to his son, but when he comes to him, he does not even wait for his son to speak. He embraces him and kisses him! I am quite sure that anyone watching this who knew the situation would be utterly dumbfounded, completely incredulous.

This is God and how He sees us. At the point where He sees us turn and begin to come to Him or come back to Him, He runs toward us, so intent on regaining that fellowship with us that His love prompts Him to sweep us up in His arms.

You see, just as the father knew that his son had learned a great deal and had "repented" by turning from that lifestyle, our heavenly Father knows and loves when we turn from the things that are meant to harm us. When we turn from them, He is able to return to us in fellowship. When we go off on our own, God is ever watchful, waiting for that sign that shows Him we are returning to Him.

There are too many people in this world who believe that that son should have beat himself up as a masochist. They believe that this somehow impresses God. Not only is God *not* impressed, but from this parable it should become clear that He does *not* want that for us.

So the son has returned, and he has a speech already prepared that he was going to say to his father. It was a self-deprecating speech designed to show his father how much he had changed and how sorry he was because of what he had done. Not only did the son realize how selfish he had been, but he knew he could not claim to be a son any longer. He would be content simply being a slave in his father's household.

We tend to approach God like this often. We think we have to prove to Him how much we recognize how bad we are and how unworthy of His love. We want to beat ourselves up and castigate ourselves, but God has other ideas.

The son truly did repent. He turned away from the lifestyle, and that was all that was necessary to be warmly received by his father.

Remember, the father saw the son from as he was far off. The father was so overjoyed that he set custom aside and ran to his son. Once he reached his son, he embraced him and kissed him. This was all done *before* the son even said anything at all. For all the father knew, his son was returning to ask for more money. Because the son had not said anything yet, how did the father know that his son had truly repented?

Of course, our heavenly Father is different than the human father in the parable. God sees our heart and knows when we turn from evil and embrace the truth.

Why do we make it so hard? Why do we insist that part of repentance must include treating ourselves as worms? This is not to say that we should ever approach God with a confident attitude about our sin. It means that we should firmly walk away from it, and in doing so, determine that we will submit ourselves to God. This can be done without all the hoopla that modern-day holiness preachers ramble on about.

Many today believe that if we are not living a lifestyle of repentance, we are not living the Christian life correctly. The trouble is that their understanding of repentance is the same as treating yourself as if you are the worst piece of scum that ever existed. This attitude must be prevalent each time sin is committed, or in their mind, true repentance has not been accomplished.

Yet we see the young man in this parable who was largely without emotion with respect to himself. The truth of the situation had prompted him to understand that he needed to change his direction. He at least knew enough about his father to believe that he would be welcomed back as a slave. Unfortunately (or maybe that's *fortunately*) for him, he did not know his father all that well, did he?

Luke 15:21
"And the son said to him, 'Father, I have sinned against heaven and in your sight; I am no longer worthy to be called your son.'"

As his father is kissing and embracing him, he starts to say the speech that he had prepared back when he was still dealing with the pigs. This was heartfelt, and he wanted it to speak to his father. He wanted his father to know that he knew his actions had not been respectful of him. He knew that he had sinned before God by treating his father in such a way. Because of that, he was prepared for the fallout. He was prepared to accept whatever punishment his father chose to give him, even if it meant he *disowned* his son. Ultimately, this is what the son expected. Being made a servant means giving up the rights of a son. He would no longer have been part of his father's family, except as a hired hand.

The son had come a long way. What began as a lifestyle based on pride and SELF finally gave way to maturity and submission to his father. The son recognized that he had done this to himself and he therefore had no one else to blame. He freely admitted to his father the fact that he had been *wrong* and then waited for the natural consequences that would follow. He was very surprised to see what those consequences were, however.

Chapter 5

Unmerited Favor

"But while he was still a long way off, his father saw him and felt compassion for him, and ran and embraced him and kissed him."
– Luke 15:20b

The father in the parable of the prodigal son reacted to his son in a way that most of us would not have done. In fact, most of us cannot even *appreciate* that particular response because it is so foreign.

Here we see the son having returned home after literally throwing away his father's money on worthless living. The son had nothing to show for it, except for the fact that the entire episode made him a great deal *wiser*. The son participated in so much waste, but there was *gain*. Having finally come to his senses, realizing that he at least would be cared for if he humbled himself enough to return home to his father, he headed out for the journey home.

Stick with me for a moment, all right, because I may be saying some things that are difficult to accept. Please understand that I'm not in the least trying to be disrespectful to God, nor am I making light of the situation. I am looking at it as honestly as I can to determine what our response to it should be.

During the process where the son sunk lower and lower until he had, in fact, hit bottom, he did not seem to care what his father thought. It's doubtful he even spent time thinking about being home and having to do all those chores. The son was living the high life now and it was his to enjoy. Then his money ran out. The fall from such a great height was nearly instantaneous. With the money gone, there was no reason for anyone to hang around him, so they moved on, looking for their next "fix" with someone else's money.

While feeding pigs, the son woke to the realization that even slaves and servants are treated better in his father's house than he was being treated now. That glimmer of truth began to work within him so that he started to realize just how wrong he had been.

While I believe there was remorse, I do *not* believe that it was the devastating kind of remorse that causes us to *freeze*, afraid to move to the right or the left. I firmly believe that this particular remorse was one of *relief*.

Let me explain. Years ago, I worked in a manufacturing plant and I was the shift supervisor for the second shift. It was my job to ensure that things in my department went smoothly.

One day we had a new hire, and right away, I didn't like him. It pains me to say that, but he just annoyed me. My attitude told him that he annoyed me too, and he could not do anything right as far as I was concerned. This went on for a few weeks, and then one day, the truth hit me. All of a sudden, I realized how I had been treating this young man!

How can I explain this? I did *not* feel terrible remorse over my sin. What I felt was terrible *sadness* for the young man! In other words, all I could think of was how terrible he must have felt having to work under me with the way I had treated him.

I did not feel a sense of *guilt*, but I felt an overwhelming sense that I had *grieved* the Lord. This was actually worse than guilt. Guilt often causes us to want to beat ourselves up emotionally. We are not good enough. We're scum. We deserve death, etc. The problem with this is that the focus is SELF. I hope I'm making sense here.

When we *grieve* over our actions, we do something different than we do when we feel overwhelming *guilt*. Guilt turns us inward. Grieving turns us outward. In other words, I *knew* that God still loved me. There was no doubt about that, but I also knew that there was this deep sense of sadness that I knew God was experiencing because of my actions. I had literally grieved the Holy Spirit and I *felt* it, and it did not feel good.

Unlike guilt, where we often wind up becoming depressed over our actions and we sit on the couch and think of how terrible we are, being *grieved* causes us to do something else. When we sense that we have *grieved* the Holy Spirit, we want to immediately make it right!

Guilt makes us feel as though we are worthless. Grieving causes us to do what we can to make it right. Guilt is what Satan uses to accuse us. If we *have* sinned, Satan goes to town on us, causing us to feel guilty about it so that we do not believe we can ever overcome, that we are destined to sink further and further into sin. We start to feel *hopeless* because of that guilt, as though there is nothing we can do.

When we grieve God, we come to understand that our actions have greatly saddened Him, and because of that we quickly want to do what we can to correct the situation. I pray that this is making sense to you.

In my case, when I realized how badly I had treated the worker on my shift, I did not feel guilty. I felt this tremendous, overpowering sadness. Yet at the same time, all I wanted to do was make it right! Guilt would have put me on the floor, curled up in the fetal position. This was far different.

Since I had decided that I was going to make things right, whatever it took, I began to feel very *glad*. I felt as though the way before me was obvious and I could not wait for the opportunity to make it right! I was actually starting to feel elated that I was going to have this opportunity to make this worker feel good about himself and what he was doing at work! I could not wait until the next day!

The next day, I made it right with that worker, and man, what a release that came with that. I had grieved the Lord, but He did not withhold His love for me at all. I knew what I had to do and was very glad to do it! It was the right thing to do.

Had I felt *guilt*, I would have had a difficult time picking myself up off the floor. I would have been overcome with feelings of worthlessness, and there are Christians who believe that this is what God wants and expects from us. I fully disagree, and the reason I am spending so much time with the prodigal son parable is because I believe that it shows quite clearly that God does not want us to beat ourselves up.

I put myself in the place of the prodigal son and because of that particular situation in my life with my co-worker, I *think* I understand what the young son felt within himself. I believe, as he started his downward slide, that he slowly began to realize that his actions were not proper. In fact, he may have come to understand that he had wronged his father, and that began to grieve him. As he allowed that to take hold of him, it naturally directed him to formulate a way to make the situation right.

In the young man's mind, he knew that he had no right to go back to his father and expect to be treated as his son. After all, he had been more than rude to his father, treating him very disrespectfully. Everyone in the neighborhood knew it. He could not deny it, and more importantly, he did not want to deny it!

I believe that from here, the knowledge of the tremendous grieving he had caused his father caused him to figure out a way to make the situation *right*. It meant that he would need to do something that he was not used to doing. It meant he would have to more than humble himself before his father.

The plan he came up with was to place his father in the obvious place of superiority, and he would do that publicly, just as he had disrespected his father publicly. He decided to submit himself to his father not as a son, but as a servant. This would say quite clearly and publicly that he (the son) understood how badly he had mistreated his father. It would also state that he knew he had no right to expect his father to treat him as a son, but would he be willing to treat him as a slave?

Doing this would show the neighbors and his father that he was sincere in wanting to give the father the respect he truly deserved. He was not doing this so that the father would feel bad for his son and take him back. He was doing it because he was sincere and wanted his father to know that he (the young son) had the utmost respect for his father. He was done demanding what he did not deserve. He was placing himself fully in his father's hands and hoping that his father would be at least willing to take him into the household as nothing more than a slave. This would restore the respect that he had stolen from his father and show that he understood the terrible consequences of his selfish actions.

I can imagine the young man starting off to his father's estate with a spring in his step. I can picture him walking quickly, wanting to make this right as soon as possible.

This was not the same young man who had left his father's home, confident, even arrogant, about his own standing in life. This young man was older, wiser, and certainly far more mature. He had come to understand responsibility and what it meant. Above all things now, he wanted his father to know that he respected him, and he was willing to show that by taking the lowest position his father could offer him.

As he stood before his father, his offer of being nothing more than a servant was absolutely sincere. He was likely emboldened to say it because of how the father kissed him and embraced him. He must have felt as though his father would be willing to make him a servant and his heart probably skipped a beat. After all, he was coming back to a completely unknown situation. His father could have ignored him, treating him as one who had died, as custom dictated. Instead, his father not only noticed him, but embraced him!

The son offers himself to his father as a servant, noting that he had treated his father horribly and did not deserve to be called his son any longer. The father, interestingly enough, would have none of that.

Luke 15:22-24
"But the father said to his slaves, 'Quickly bring out the best robe and put it on him, and put a ring on his hand and sandals on his feet; and bring the fattened calf, kill it, and let us eat and celebrate; for this son of mine was dead and has come to life again; he was lost and has been found.' And they began to celebrate."

Wow, did you read that? Go back and read it again. Notice that the father completely *ignores* what the son is offering. He doesn't even dignify his son's preposterous offer with a reply. Instead he does something else, something the son never expected. He treated his son like royalty!

The son barely gets his request out when the father immediately turns to his slaves nearby and orders them to:

1. *Bring out the best robe*
2. *Put that robe on the son*
3. *Put a ring on his hand*
4. *Put sandals on his feet*
5. *Get the fattened calf and kill it*
6. *Prepare to celebrate!*

Who would have expected such a response? I would not have, would you? The father – in front of his slaves – makes a very bold and public declaration by doing all of these things. He is saying to everyone that this young man is *not* nor will *ever* be considered a slave! He is my son and everyone will treat him as my son!

Make no mistake, the young son was given royal status that day, something he did not deserve and something he never would have imagined. He had gone off on his own, used and wasted his father's money, done his own thing, lived his own life of immorality, likely never even sending his father a postcard, and when he was done living that life, he returned home.

For the father to be able to receive his son like that tells us something about God. It tells us that God loves us, more than we can understand now. He loves us with a love that is hard for us to truly appreciate. When we expect Him to beat us down emotionally (as we believe we deserve), God comes through with love that draws us closer to Him.

Let me ask a question here. Which teaches you more about true love, grace or law?

Many people believe that when we return to God after going off on our own to enjoy sin for a season (however small that season might be), we should come crawling back to Him, beating ourselves with a whip. This shows God just how bad we feel, as though He is incapable of reading our heart.

Not long ago, I saw a picture on the 'Net of a group of young Muslim men involved in a ritual of cutting themselves as some form of penance. This apparently proves to Allah that they are serious about wanting to please that god.

Do you recall the situation on Mt. Carmel with Elijah and the 450 prophets of Baal (cf. 1 Kings 18:17-40)? It was here that we see the prophets cutting themselves to gain Baal's attention so that he would respond to them. It didn't work, and all they got from the skies was silence.

Penance is a large part of some of the major religions. It is part of Catholicism, Islam, Buddhism, and others. It is nothing more than an effort by humans to convince God that they are sorry for their sins. If they can convince God that they are really, *really* sorry by inflicting pain and drawing blood, then God will be impressed enough to bless them. Unfortunately, an aspect of this has infiltrated the visible Church, and people are often legalistic about how we should approach God and what our relationship with Him should be.

Does God want us to harm ourselves, even emotionally, in order to prove to Him that we are terribly sorry for what we have done? Is He somehow impressed with this? I don't see that in Scripture, yet others do.

The prodigal son is a story of two young men (we will get to the older son shortly) who obviously do not know their own father, though they certainly think they do. It is this misunderstanding of their father that prompts their wrong and even harmful attitudes.

What we see in the father's approach to *both* of his sons is a stalwart love and acceptance of them, something that is often missing among Christians today in their relationship with one another and with God.

Let's face it, if we believe God expects us to treat ourselves poorly over our sin, wouldn't that same attitude extend itself to others in the visible Church? Wouldn't we wind up becoming judgmental and legalistic to one another under the guise of "honoring" or "revering" God?

This is completely pharisaic in our approach, and because of it this is not what God wants for us. If the parable of the prodigal son is any indication at all, it is obviously *not* the way God treats us. We need to understand that as difficult as it can be, we must strive to realize that God is love and exercises that love to all people, but especially to those within His family. While people live, God's love is being extended to them. If they wind up dying without ever receiving that love in the form of His salvation, they can expect to be on the receiving end of His wrath for all eternity. Why would anyone take that chance by ignoring His love now?

Chapter 6

The Older Son's Legalism

"For so many years I have been serving you and I have never neglected a command of yours." – Luke 15:29b

The older son is a bit of a seeming conundrum. On one hand, he seems devoted to his father, doing what is required and never complaining about it. On the other hand, he seems to be harboring deep resentment toward his father.

It's interesting, but if we were to simply judge the older son by outward appearances, we would have to say that he is loyal to a fault and a very hard worker. We would have to say that the older son worked hard for his father, and we might even be tempted to think that the older son in the parable of the prodigal son of Luke 15 loved and respected his father.

This, of course, is based on *outward* appearances. It simply proves that we often do not really know people at all. While we *think* we might, it can literally take years to really get to know someone.

Waving a quick "hello" or exchanging momentary pleasantries to your neighbor does not allow you to get to know that person or them to get to know you. How many times have we heard or read that someone in some household went ballistic and killed family members and then took his own life? The normal reaction with few exceptions by the people in that area is something along the lines of, *"They seemed like a nice family. The father worked hard around the house and the kids seemed happy."* After a while, you begin to wonder about all the "quiet" people on your block. Are they merely waiting to explode one day?

We've already gone over the bulk of this passage from Luke, detailing the young son and looking somewhat at the father (though we will deal more deeply with him in an upcoming chapter). While all the hoopla was going on back at the ranch because of the young son's return, true to form, the older son was hard at work in the fields.

Luke 15:25-26
"Now his older son was in the field, and when he came and approached the house, he heard music and dancing. And he summoned one of the servants and began inquiring what these things could be."

The above two verses highlight the first sign of potential trouble since the young son has returned. Let's consider things from the older son's perspective for a moment.

First, like his younger brother (presumably), the older son did the work that their father set before them each day. It did not appear as though the older son complained but simply did what was asked of him to do. Outwardly, there did not appear to be a problem between father and son.

One day, the older son hears or learns that the younger son basically took his inheritance and stormed off the set! He was off to see the world and to ultimately spend his money foolishly.

I'm thinking that the older son was probably a bit perturbed at this, not that the younger son had left, but that he left *with* his inheritance! This would likely become like a burr under the older son's saddle that would keep bothering him until it grew into a mountain of anger.

On one hand, the older son may have been glad that the younger son had left. Maybe they didn't get along, and it is very likely that the younger son had a habit of complaining. It is doubtful that one day, out of the blue, completely contrary to the way he thought and lived, that the younger son all of a sudden developed a case of *"I've gotta get out of here!"* outlook on life.

Chances are good that the younger son had been contemplating this move for some time and may have even shared his desire with his older brother. Who knows? The reality is that the day came, the young son demanded and got his inheritance, and then he took off, theoretically for good.

Much to his dismay, the younger son had gone off to sow some wild oats but had now returned. That was galling. While his younger brother had gallivanted off to places unknown for good times, the older son remained and continued his life of working hard for his father with a stiff upper lip. Then one day, he hears and sees a commotion back at the house and learns from one of the servants what had happened.

Luke 15:27
"And he said to him, 'Your brother has come, and your father has killed the fattened calf because he has received him back safe and sound.'"

Wow, that must have been *great* news! Whoopee! The young upstart who had demanded his inheritance and run off to be Mr.

Playboy is now back. Safe and sound? Who cares! He was the one who ran off. He wasn't kidnapped! Why should I – the older son – be excited that my brother ran out of money and came back for more?

This did not set well at all with the older brother. We know that from the very next verse.

Luke 15:28

"But he became angry and was not willing to go in; and his father came out and began pleading with him."

All of the pent-up anger that the older brother had kept in check started coming out. The older son began pouting and would not go in to welcome his brother back home.

As human beings, we can definitely appreciate and even relate to the older brother's attitude here. We know it is wrong, but we can relate to it because there have possibly been times in our lives when we have acted just like that when we felt cheated and underappreciated.

The older son became resolute in refusing to obey his father here. He believed that he had a good and legitimate reason to put his foot down. He believed that his brother had gotten from his father what he had not deserved, and here was his brother back again; would his father respond much the same way?

What if young brother arrived at the same point again, deciding that staying home was just too *servile,* and wanted to sow some more wild oats? What would his father do if that situation arose again, give him *yet more* money to throw away?

The older brother had a point, but he also failed to see things from an accurate perspective. In some ways, the older son is very much like a legalist.

The older son slaved away for his father, and he probably did consider his work "slaving." He never *outwardly* complained that we are aware of, simply doing what he was asked to do.

Unlike his younger brother, he had never disrespected his father. He never brought shame to the family that way. As far as the neighbors and the community in general knew, the older brother was an upstanding member of the family.

Not the younger brother. Oh no, he wasn't happy doing what he was supposed to do. No, he needed to have his money *now*, so that he could live the high life *now,* and who cared about the father or his older brother? The younger brother represented the height of arrogance and self-centeredness! Yet here he was, back "safe and sound." Who cares? The older brother may have hoped to never see his younger brother again.

I can picture the older brother absolutely *fuming* upon hearing the news that his younger brother had returned. Let's not miss the specific wording of the servant, either. He specifically said that the young brother was "safe and sound." In doing so, that servant had completely understood that the young son had been fully restored to the family as a son, and because of it he was obligated to treat him with respect, whether or not the servant thought he deserved it or not. In fact, it was not that servant's place to determine a person's worth. His job was to follow orders and do what was expected of him by his employer.

When the older son became thoroughly obstinate after hearing the news of his younger brother's return, he simply refused to go into the house to become part of the celebration. The older brother had not been there with his father as the younger son approached. The older son had not seen his father's response to the young son even as he was still approaching. Neither had the older brother been there to actually hear what his younger brother had confessed to their father.

For all the older brother knew, the younger brother may have simply waltzed up with a quick, "*I'm BACK!*" and expected everything to return to the way it had been prior to his leaving. The older brother really knew none of this, but his angry reaction tells us that he had been carrying his anger around for some time. Now it came boiling out, in spite of the fact that his father was actually *pleading* with his older son to come to the house and join the festivities.

In essence, it was the older son's turn to disrespect his father, and he was doing so *loudly* and in front of the servants. Let's look and see what the older son said to his father.

Luke 15:29-30
"But he answered and said to his father, 'Look! For so many years I have been serving you and I have never neglected a command of yours; and yet you have never given me a young goat, so that I might celebrate with my friends; but when this son of yours came, who has devoured your wealth with prostitutes, you killed the fattened calf for him.'"

Wow, talk about pent up feelings. Right away, the older son starts in by ticking off all the things he had done for his father.

1. *Served the father for years*
2. *Never neglected a command*
3. *Never received a young goat to celebrate*

Look folks, you don't have that information on the tip of your tongue unless it's been rolling around in your mind for quite some time. I imagine that this older son often thought about all the things he did for his father and all the times he never failed to achieve what his father expected him to do. He was a tremendous son and very faithful. What did he get in return? Nothing. Zilch. Zippo, not even a young goat so he could have a party with his friends. It was obvious to the older son that his father had absolutely no concern for him.

Then he starts railing on his younger brother accusing him of

1. *Devouring the father's wealth*
2. *Paying for prostitutes*
3. *Being rewarded for evil with the fattened calf*

We do not know if in truth the young son actually had prostitutes. He certainly could have because of the use of the world "immoral" in the text with reference to the lifestyle of the young son after he left home. We just don't know that for sure. It appears as though the older son is simply accusing the older brother without knowing any facts. Then again, maybe the young brother had bragged that this is what he wanted to do if he ever had the chance to leave. Again, we just do not know so we can't be dogmatic about it. We must simply leave it knowing that the way the young son lived was immoral.

Of course, we see what the older son is doing. He is puffing himself up while denigrating his brother. At the same time, he is continuing to disrespect his father by *taking his father to task* for the way he treated the younger son.

He is basically saying to the father, "*What is the matter with you? Are you stupid? You give this son his undeserved inheritance and he runs off and spends it on floozies and drink!*" In essence, the older son was castigating his father by questioning his decisions. He had become as disrespectful to his father (in a different way) as his younger brother had been. There was no difference between these two. However, the young brother, as we have pointed out, learned something that forever changed his opinion of his father. It's too bad it cost the father what it cost him, but in the end, the father had truly gained a son. The older son, though, was not to be placated. He believed he had a case against his brother *and* against the father for his ridiculous decision in first, allowing the young son to leave with as much money as he had given him, and second, allowing him to now return. He might as well have called his father a fool.

Luke 15:31-32

"And he said to him, 'Son, you have always been with me, and all that is mine is yours. But we had to celebrate and rejoice, for this brother of yours was dead and has begun to live, and was lost and has been found.'"

The above text helps us understand where the father is coming from, not that he was required to explain it to anyone. However, in telling this parable to the crowd, Jesus wanted them to see the inner workings of all three individuals because they all have something to say, something very important. It was by these three individuals that Jesus wanted the people to understand who God is and how He sees us.

In the days of Jesus, everyone would have agreed that both of these sons were initially terrible for the way they treated their father. The father had every right to leave them out of his will and leave everything to one of his faithful servants instead. In fact, people would have quite possibly expected the father to do that and may have been a bit unclear as to why he did not.

The father is going far beyond what he needed to do here. He actually takes the time to explain to the older son *why* the older son should come in and celebrate with everyone. He assured his older son that he *knew* that the older son had always acted responsibly. He knew that the older son was someone he could always count on to get things done.

The father even goes further by saying, "*Look son, whatever I have is yours!*" What is the father saying here? He is clearly stating that the older son *could* have asked for a young goat and it would have been given to him so that he could celebrate with his friends.

Why didn't the older son ever ask? He did not ask simply because he did not *like* his father. The older son completely misunderstood his relationship with his father. While the older son saw himself as a slave and saw his father as a taskmaster, the father saw his son as loyal and someone he could count on. Why the older son had never asked for anything was not something he understood, but it actually made the father love the older son more.

Unfortunately, we learn from this situation that *both* sons turned out to be prodigals. The younger son actually physically left his father's estate while the older son remained. However, the older son was also gone – *emotionally*. They had both left.

While the younger son dreamt of the day when he would be free of his father's shackles, able to spend his inheritance on whatever he wanted, the older son probably dreamt of the same thing! The difference is that only one of the sons left the estate physically, but both had long ago left the estate emotionally.

This leaves us with an interesting question. The young son left, learned a very valuable lesson, and returned, humbled and ready to do whatever his father needed. He returned with only one hopeful expectation: that his father would take him back as a servant.

He never in a million years expected his father to react to him as he had done. Though he in no way deserved it, his father actually put a robe on him, placed a ring on his finger, and gave him sandals! He heard him give the order to kill the fattened calf in order to celebrate the young son's return.

The young son was in awe. He was probably speechless, and because of this, all he could do was love his father. He had finally understood that all those years his father had truly loved him, but he was too blind to see it! He had spent so much time and energy feeling sorry for his plight that he had never understood exactly how his father viewed him.

Here he was, back at the ranch, and he was being treated like royalty, in spite of the way he had despicably treated his father. The interesting thing here is that this entire situation *could* have caused him to once again focus on himself. He could have begun contemplating just how evil his thoughts and actions had been. He could have argued with his father about the way his father had received him back, saying he didn't deserve it and he simply wanted to be a slave.

Instead, he was dumbfounded, in awe of how much his father loved him. How could he have missed that before?

As he focused on his father's love for him, as opposed to how he had sinned against his father, something happened. He began to understand that it is love that draws people and endears them to another. It is not work for the sake of work. It was love that crafted an everlasting bond that nothing could break.

Oh, you can bet that this young son would work for his father as he had never worked. He would appreciate everything about his father and how much his father had simply *forgiven*. How could he *ever* repay his father for such love? He knew he could not. He also knew that he would *never* treat his father with disdain again.

The young son was a changed man. He had encountered true and lasting love, love that accepted, love that received. The young son knew beyond doubt that the love that his father had exhibited toward him that day would not go unnoticed. He would endeavor to spend the rest of his life showing his father how much he in turn loved *him*. He would glory in it and would actually look for opportunities to show his father this love.

Unfortunately, the same could not be said of the older brother. While the younger brother had taken off, the older brother had stayed, dutifully fulfilling all the responsibilities that were placed on him without a verbal question.

However, in his heart, the older brother was far from his father. He did what he did with a deep sense of *legalism*. He did it because he *had* to do it. He completed the work given to him because he was expected to complete it. Those were the reasons why he did what he did.

The older son never did anything for his father simply because he loved him. He did what he did because that was "the law" of the house. Those were his marching orders, and he made sure to do what he was told. Unfortunately, his heart was so far from his father that he never realized that he could have done those things for his father not out of legalism, but out of love. Had he done so, his life would have been easier, his work load lighter, and the results of his work would have been far more beneficial.

It was the *exact same* work, but with a different attitude, an attitude that would have made all the difference in the world. It was this attitude that was now deeply resident within the young son and something he would carry with him for the remainder of his life.

He had not returned home with demands, the way he had left. While he left in a cloud of arrogance, he came home in the dust of humility. The father's reaction to his younger son fully opened his eyes to the meaning of a father's love for his son. Now the son knew that if he made a mistake, the father would be quick to forgive upon the confession of the son. Now the young son knew that his father was the best representation of God's character that he had ever encountered. His father lived a life of love, and he also wanted to exemplify that trait for however long he lived!

The older son went back to the field, angry, alone, and remaining legalistic. He would continue to work for his father and he would continue to never ask for anything. He would show his father what loyalty meant. He would prove to his father that he "loved" him because he would continue to fulfill every one of his father's commands without fail.

What the father wanted far more than that was his son's *heart*. This is something he had with the younger son, but not with the older. Though part of the family, he was really not part of the family, because he failed to understand the true nature of his father's character.

The older son viewed his father as a wicked taskmaster and reacted to him that way. The older son saw his father as he truly was: kind, compassionate, and loving.

Let me ask you. Which trait is more attractive? Which trait causes you to *want* to do things for the father?

Why do we still believe that as Christians, we must toe the line and prove to God how much we love him, keeping a stiff upper lip and digging in to complete whatever He gives us?

I am very aware of passages from the book of James and elsewhere that speak about the fact that faith without works is dead. This is true, and nothing I have stated in this book is meant to negate that.

Because the son learned how much his father loved him, that realization prompted him to want to live a life that *pleased* his father. He did not take his father's loving reaction to his return as a sign that he could now sit on the couch and play video games all day! He saw love in action and it *affected* him deeply. He would choose to respond to his father in love and would simply show that love to his father every day by doing the things that would make his father's life *easier*.

This is what it means to live the Christian life. If we say we are a Christian but we live as if we are not, then it is seriously doubtful that we are, in fact, a Christian at all. Claiming to be a Christian and living a life that caters to SELF are diametrically opposed to one another. It is impossible. If we love Him, we will serve Him. It is that simple. The older son never learned that, while the younger son *did*.

Chapter 7

He Saw, Agreed, and Changed

"But when he came to his senses, he said, 'How many of my father's hired men have more than enough bread, but I am dying here with hunger!" – Luke 15:17

I woke up today and did what I normally do. I headed downstairs, grabbed a cup of coffee and walked out to the back patio. There, I opened the Word and read. After that, I prayed, and then I prayed some more.

The thing I find fascinating is that with each new day, I realize that it is one more day that the Lord has given me. The question is, to what purpose?

Since the Lord has indeed given me one more day, it is patently clear that He has specific things He wants me to do in this day, otherwise there is no point in providing me another day.

This day, like any other day, is His day. It is a gift to me, but only so that I can submit myself to Him. The question of each day becomes, *"Lord, what do you want me to do today?"*

As I look back over my life, I see too many days I lived with my own goals in mind. I spent time planning things, doing things, and enjoying things that were fine in and of themselves, but my focus was wrong. Rather than considering what I would do each day, I should have been thinking about what God wanted me to do with each of those days. After all, He gave them to me. My days - like everyone else's days - are fully numbered. If that is the case, how can I possibly squander the days I am given?

So with the start of each new day, I wait before Him. I ask Him to guide me for that day, to fulfill the things He would have me do, for the sake of His Name and for His glory.

Not once have I ever "heard" Him provide me audible directions for my life. But it is important that if I'm going to pray at all, faith must accompany that prayer, believing that if I am asking Him to guide me then He will do it, whether I hear His voice or not. No, I do not expect to hear His voice. I expect that He will simply guide my steps.

With respect to the young son in the parable of the prodigal son, I have noted the attitude of the young son *and* the father, two remarkably different individuals. I have pointed out how the son at first was so proud and arrogant that he had the audacity to demand from his father the inheritance that would be his *after* his father died! Not only was this absolutely disrespectful, selfish, and arrogant, but the young son did not care how neighbors would look at that situation. The young son's eyes were focused solely on himself, his wants, his perceived needs, and his desires. He did not care what his "request" did to his father.

The interesting thing is that this young man was already part of the family. This was his father. As a son, he had far more rights and privileges than any hired hand or servant on his father's estate. None of that was good enough, and I am willing to bet that the young son did not really notice any of that. He was too busy listening to the dictates of SELF. The only thing that was important was what *he* wanted, what *he* felt he was owed.

It is interesting to also note how quickly the father gave his son what the son demanded. Without hesitation, the father gave his son his inheritance, and without so much as a "*thanks Dad!*" the son was off on a journey to begin his new life, unfettered from the demands of his father.

We need to realize that this son was not married. He did not have responsibilities to a wife or children, which would have understandably caused his loyalties to be primarily with them. In this case, the son was single, and he wanted to live the single, immoral life. In the text of Luke 15, we are simply told that the son went off and lived an immoral life, squandering the money that he had received from his father. We are left to guess what it is that he did that was immoral.

Fortunately for the son, in due time - when he ran out of money, his so-called friends had deserted him, and he had found a job feeding pigs - he came to his senses, and I do not believe that was by chance. He began to realize the kind of man his father had been toward him and his brother. He began to see that in spite of the way he had treated his father, he was a very fair man. He treated all of his servants fairly and kindly and always made sure that they had enough to eat.

He then realized that if this was how his father had treated the servants, *maybe* he would be willing to take him back not as a son, but as a servant! At least this way he would have a full stomach. The son realized that expecting his father to receive him back as a son was asking too much.

I absolutely love the transformation that occurs within the son. He comes up with a plan - one that comes from the *heart*. Because he had treated his father like garbage publicly, he would apologize to his father sincerely and also publicly. He would submit himself to his father, asking only that he be treated as a servant because he had grown to understand that he was no longer worthy to be called his father's son.

Yes, that was what he would do! I can imagine how free the son felt at this point. Some might argue that he was feeling terrible remorse and guilt, and that's the way it should be. I disagree because when we feel guilty, the focus is on ourselves. In other words, we begin to see how wrong we were, which is good. But the problem comes in when that's all we see, and then we start to beat ourselves up emotionally for being so despicable. This is what guilt does. It simply *accuses* and offers absolutely no solution whatsoever. It turns our focus inward and leaves it there.

I believe that while the son without doubt absolutely realized how wrong he was, because he came up with a plan to *correct that wrong* as much as possible, he was not feeling guilt at all, but *freedom*! Let me explain. *Guilt* tends to immobilize a person, causing that person to often sink to the lowest level possible as they castigate themselves. Oh, we can't beat on ourselves enough!

However, when we *grieve* God, causing Him pain, the freedom that comes from realizing how to *fix* the problem we created because of our sin is actually *exhilarating*. This is far from "earning" our salvation. It is doing what we should be doing because we see the wrong we have committed and we want to make it right, as far as we are able.

I can imagine the son left that filthy pig pen in the parable for his father's estate with a quick gait. He had a purpose. He was probably very much looking forward to making things right with his father. He had no guarantees, though, that his father would even acknowledge him because of what he had done, but it was worth a try.

I can also imagine that this young man began to pray and might have prayed the entire journey. I believe it was God who opened his eyes in the first place, and because of that he now felt emboldened to speak with God. Who knows how long it had been since that young son had taken the time to open his heart to the God of his father?

On this journey back home, I can imagine that he spent a good portion of the walk just *confessing* his sin and attitude to God. I don't believe he did this because he *felt* guilty or terrible. He knew he *was* guilty whether he felt it or not. That was simply a fact that he could no longer deny. He agreed with God wholeheartedly that he was guilty, that he was not worthy of being called his father's son.

I can see in my mind's eye this young man's prayer that may have gone a bit like this: "*O God of my father, though I am not worthy to be heard by you, I pray that you would incline your ear to me. I have wronged my father and sinned in your sight. I am not worthy of being called my father's son. I have no right to ask you for anything, yet I pray that should you be willing, please allow my father to receive me not as a son, but as a servant! I have deliberately and with malice treated my father with tremendous disrespect. I know that this is wrong, but I'm asking you, Lord, for the opportunity to make it right! Help me to submit myself to my father for whatever it is he believes is the right thing to do with and for me. I am sorry for how I have hurt him and how I have dragged your holy Name through the mud. Please, bless my father more than you already have done. Help him to see my absolute sincerity. Help me to work to regain his trust. It may sound hollow, but I do love you, Lord. You know my heart. I thank you for opening my eyes to the truth. I thank you for showing me just how wrong I have been. I thank you, Lord, that though you could have cast me off or even killed me, you chose not to do so. My father was right about you, Lord. You are endlessly patient and loving when you do not need to be. I cannot thank you enough for that, Lord. Help me to bring glory to your Name out of this mess that I have created. I pray that you will be blessed in and through me. Amen."*

Of course, I have no idea *what* he prayed or *if* the young man prayed at all. However, I cannot imagine the time he spent journeying back to his father after his eyes were opened *not* spent with God in prayer.

Some would undoubtedly say that this man should have *crawled* the entire way back on his knees in order to really prove to God that he was penitent. That's garbage, in my view. God already saw the young man's heart and He knew what was there. God saw the *proof* of the change that had come over the young man because God Himself precipitated that change. Did He need to see tears of guilt? Did God require tremendous feelings of self-deprecation in order to be impressed enough with the young man to turn His attention to him? Not when God was the One who caused the change to begin with and saw the effect that occurred. The prodigal had turned around and was moving *away* from his sin.

There is a church in Mexico City in which parishioners literally crawl on their knees from the back of that church to the front on the hard, rough concrete. By the time they reach the front of that church, their knees are skinned, bruised and bleeding. The only people they are impressing are those who see their misery and themselves. They believe this proves to God that they are truly repentant. *"See how I am making myself feel, God? Do you notice my self-inflicted pain and misery? See Lord, I really am repentant!"*

Whether we emotionally beat ourselves up or physically harm ourselves, the only purpose it seems to serve is to prove either to ourselves or to those who see our pain that we are truly sincere. Unfortunately, I don't believe we have proven anything to God except that we are still trying to use SELF to please Him. It won't work. It is anathema to Him.

We need to notice, with respect to the young man, that there is no indication that he shed tears of guilt or self-judgment. He may have shed tears of *joy* because of the release that came from this new awareness, but it seems pretty clear that he did not castigate himself or beat himself up. He did not throw himself to the ground of that pigsty, wallowing in self-pity and self-denigration, crying out to anyone who would notice how terrible he was and how he deserved to die.

On the contrary, the young man did a number of things that proved to God he had changed:

1. *saw* the truth
2. came to the *realization* of what that truth *meant*
3. *changed* his direction
4. *determined* to set things right

Those four steps that I have just noted are the very things that constitute *repentance*. It can be as simple and as heartfelt as that because God sees what goes on in our *heart*. He does not need to see anything else. No outward display ever substitutes for the honesty of the heart. While we *may* be given to tears because of the sorrow we have caused, it should serve to move us toward the goal of righting the situation. If you are *not* brought to tears, you should not condemn yourself because of it. Everyone reacts differently.

I have grown tired of those who push their definition of "holiness" on me and other individuals who at times are hurting under the tremendous load of enemy-inspired *guilt*. These individuals believe that if you don't walk around with an affected, ethereal-sounding voice and constantly use self-denigrating speech, along with always being on the verge of tears due to realizing just how sinful and terrible you truly are, then you have not truly repented. The interesting thing with these people is that I note how judgmental and even condemning they often are. They group all "Christians" together, making no distinction between those who *are* Christians and those who only *say* they are Christians.

In effect, and unfortunately, many of these individuals appear to me to be self-serving. They give the impression they are holy and they seem to spread a message of holiness, when in my opinion, what they are actually spreading is a message of guilt – *paralyzing*, *denigrating*, *guilt*. I do not believe God uses guilt on those who belong to His family. While He most certainly *will* use guilt on those who are *not* His, it is Satan who uses guilt on God's children. He uses guilt to condemn, choke, and extinguish. He wields guilt as a weapon to destroy our faith in a loving God.

Romans 8 starts by telling us we are no longer condemned, and it ends with the fact that nothing can separate us from God's love. How does *guilt* fit into that picture? It doesn't. You cannot sandwich guilt in between no condemnation and never being separated from His love! God *will* chastise us as our parent, but He will never *guilt* us into doing or believing something.

As a parent (if you are one), do you spent your time trying to make your kids feel guilty about the way they treat you or what they are doing wrong in general? Do you use guilt cues as a mainstay, causing within your kids tremendous exasperation so that they wind up doing things for you out of duty instead of love and respect? If you do, then you need to know that this is not the way God treats His children and it is not the way He treats you, if you belong to Him.

Feeling guilty about something has no place in the walk of an authentic Christian. When we are wrong, God will let us know, and most of the time we will know *immediately*. It is in our best interests to react as the young son reacted. He *saw*, he *agreed*, and he *changed* direction. It's as simple as that, but that doesn't satisfy some within the field of evangelism. They want to *see* your pain because if they don't see it, then they doubt your repentance is genuine. Who are *they* to demand what God Himself does *not* demand? They are not the ones who need to see your repentance, unless, of course, they believe that they have the power to absolve you of your sin. It is *God* who needs to see it.

The prodigal son gives us a picture of what actual repentance looks like. It is essentially seeing the truth and acting on that truth. If the realization of that truth brings tears of joy to your eyes, then that is wonderful. If it makes you want to shout "*glory to God!*" excellent. If it makes you want to *hurt* yourself emotionally or physically, then it is WRONG!

In the next chapter, we will talk about the father's reaction to his son's *return*. Join me for that, all right? In the meantime, ask the Lord what He has for you to do *today*. How are you to bring glory to Him today? How will He work in and through you *today*? He has something specific for you if you are one of His children. He will likely *not* send you a message via courier, nor will you hear voices in your head. As you read His Word and pray, He will give you the grace to know that He is leading you throughout the day. The things that you have viewed as mundane will take on greater meaning.

As you move through the day, His discernment will allow you to see things that you might have otherwise missed. There's a person who is hurting that you can help. You remember that you need to pray for someone. You gain more wisdom from His Word today than you thought possible. It was easier to memorize Scripture. Your entire outlook for the day is seen from His perspective, not yours.

As authentic Christians, we are blessed with the only God who has chosen to live *within* us in order *recreate* us into the image of His Son. The Lord reigns, and the more time we spend with Him the more we begin to realize that He does reign, and more than anything, we want to serve Him. I hope and pray that this is your life today. The Lord *is* with you, if you are His. May He open your eyes to that truth as you seek to serve Him this day.

Chapter 8

The Father's Unfailing Love

"Son, you have always been with me, and all that is mine is yours."
– Luke 15:31

The father's love for his two sons never failed. It almost seems that he doted on them, but it clear from the attitudes of the sons themselves that this could not have been the case. The two sons seemed to see their father as a taskmaster and not a loving father. We can only wonder why this was the case, but the reality is that Jesus was presenting a parable that would adequately explain to His listening crowd the unfailing love of God the Father in terms that the average person could understand.

The father in the parable seemed to remain in the background, though it is obvious that his presence was certainly felt by the two sons. They had come to a point where they had grown to quite possibly hate their father. At the very least, they had strong negative feelings toward him that we learned were simply not accurate.

The father in the parable represents God the Father. It is interesting in any number of ways to look at the father's reaction to his sons and realize that this is how God reacts toward us. First of all, God is no respecter of persons, causing the rain to fall on the just and unjust (cf. Acts 10:34-35; Romans 2:11). As God, He and He alone creates people with certain gifts and abilities, and this is in spite of the fact that many will never come to know Him. God provides success for people regardless of their relationship to Him.

The father in the parable treated his sons fairly, though they did not see it that way. The father expected them to fulfill certain obligations, and they came to see these obligations as chains around their necks.

It is likely that the father in the parable put up with a great deal of attitude from his sons, yet he likely overlooked it because of his great love for his sons. The father in the parable seemed to love his sons with an undying love, yet they did not realize it at all.

In the parable, the father never seems pushy at all. He never denounces his sons or ever seems to chastise them at all. Yet the sons come to know their father as a hard man, one who expects a great deal from them.

It is clear that the sons overreacted to their father. Though he loved them, they could not see it, and the reason they did not see it was because they had their eyes solely on themselves.

SELF has a way of deceiving us into thinking that we are getting the raw end of the deal. SELF wants to be supreme, yet it will never be that. SELF wants us to deny anything that does not please SELF. God knows that this creates nothing but sadness and gloom. Ultimately, if we follow SELF to the end, we find ourselves in the same place where all sin ends up: the Lake of Fire. In the end, SELF wants to destroy us, yet we rarely realize that.

If we look back at the time of Adam and Eve, we realize a number of things that they apparently came to ignore about God. In Genesis 2:8, we learn how easily God approached them. *"And they heard the sound of the Lord God walking in the garden in the cool of the day."*

Adam and Eve had both just sinned. It appeared that it was the habit of God to literally walk and talk with the two, teaching them things about His Creation as well as simply fellowshipping with them.

We also learn that it was cool in the Garden of Eden. The temperature was optimal and very pleasant. I can picture a very serene, enjoyable scene in the garden every day.

Yet we also know that this was not enough for Adam and Eve. They fell prey to the temptation to believe that they were actually tethered to God's chain. If they wanted to be truly free, then they would have to exercise their free will to set themselves free from God and His dictates.

In reality, Satan had very little with which to work. The only thing at his disposal was the tree of knowledge of good and evil. That was it, and he made the best use of it that he could in order to push his agenda.

Consider the fact that though Adam and Eve enjoyed the splendor of an exquisite garden, literally flowing with milk and honey, Satan found a way to distract them from that so that he could get them to focus on the *downside* of that paradise. The downside, of course, was the one tree that they were not allowed to eat from, and it is that tree that grew to gall them.

It is interesting to see how easily human beings can be swayed to think wrongly of a situation. While Adam and Eve were in the best possible world, Satan found a way to make it seem as though there was something *better*. He is not called the Tempter for nothing.

If Adam and Eve both succumbed to the temptation to focus on the one negative amidst all the positives, it is any wonder that the two sons in the parable of the prodigal son did the same? Those two sons were *already* fallen. They were born with the sin nature.

It really doesn't take much to sidetrack people so that they wind up going off in a direction that is opposed to God. People debate and argue about things all the time, and they do it with vehemence because they truly believe their position.

Think about what people can argue about. Whether people are discussing politics, religion, or sports, opinions are strong and tempers can flare.

For the two sons, they likely gave attention to their own thoughts. The tempter wasted no time in telling these boys how bad their lives were and how much better they could be.

Maybe the boys began to show signs of exasperation with their father and maybe the father ignored those signs, believing them to be a passing phase. Maybe it got to a point where there was little laughter between father and sons because the relationship had become solely focused on work and chores.

I like to think that the father greatly loved his sons and wished they could see it. He never "rode their cases," as we might say. Though he expected that they complete their assigned tasks, he knew that one day they would have complete charge over the entire estate, and he wanted them to be prepared for that. It wasn't simply a matter of using his sons as you would use a slave. They needed to learn everything about the workings of his farm. They needed to know it inside and out. Yes, they were helping out a great deal, but one day they would appreciate it when they took over the reins of the father's operation. The father, more than anything, wished they could see that. It would give them a sense of ownership.

I'm sure the father noticed the emotional distance between him and his sons. Unfortunately, that distance was due solely to their unrealistic expectations.

Because of those unrealistic expectations, the two sons did not see what the father saw. Instead they simply saw a situation in which they were one of their father's hired hands, servants to do the father's bidding. Indeed, their hearts were far from their father.

They did everything the father wanted them to do, but they did it in a cold, calculating way. This is so reminiscent of the way many within the nation of Israel treated God.

In Isaiah 29:13, we read these haunting words: *"Because this people draw near with their words And honor Me with their lip service, But they remove their hearts far from Me, And their reverence for Me consists of tradition learned by rote."*

Jesus says pretty much the same thing in Matthew 15:8, where He quotes the above passage from Isaiah. The truth of the matter was that though the people *did* what they were *supposed* to do, as God says to Isaiah, the hearts of the people were not in it at all. They had reduced worship of God to a type of work that they were able to do without even thinking about it (rote).

Because of this attitude the people of Israel had toward God, they wound up dishonoring Him routinely. This was one of the biggest reasons that God at times sent another nation to overcome Israel and bring them into captivity. God of course knew that eventually these people who had been ignoring Him would begin to call out to Him once again.

God chose chastisement as a means of regaining the honor that He deserved from the people and nation He had created. Because of new generations, though, it was not long before that new generation would begin to emotionally move away from God and dabble in idolatry until it often overwhelmed them and completely pushed God out. Even so, the people continued the practice of worshiping God with their lips, even when their hearts were not in it.

In many ways, this is how both sons reacted toward their father. They did what was expected of them because that is what good sons did. They didn't like it, and it most likely showed in their attitudes toward their father.

Yet the father continued to love both sons. When the young son came and demanded his inheritance, it was another way of the young son saying to his father, *"I wish you were dead and I am treating you as if you are dead by asking for my inheritance."* I cannot imagine as a parent what that would feel like, but I'm sure it would not feel good at all.

The father gave his son what he demanded but did not deserve. He gave him his inheritance, likely knowing full well that the son would leave to sow wild oats and ignore his upbringing. The father opted to do two things he probably did not want to do. First, he gave his son what the son demanded, and second, he allowed his son to leave.

This is God's graciousness to us. He sometimes gives us what He knows is not best for us because it can teach us the truth about ourselves and God. He allows us to go where He might not want us to go because of the potential outcome.

It is not unusual for me to receive nasty or sarcastic notes from atheists because of the things I write on my blog at www.studygrowknowblog. Often it seems as though these individuals go out of their way to castigate me for my beliefs and opinions when they could simply ignore it. When they do submit a response to one of my blogs, if they have a point I'll often post it, even if they are being extremely arrogant and petty.

My wish for them is that they will come to see the truth. God's desire for them is that they will forsake their atheism and come to Him for salvation. What always amazes me about atheists is that they are so sure that God does not exist. Yet when you ask them to prove it to you, they will tell you without hesitation that you cannot prove a negative.

When they respond like this, they simply do not realize that they are contradicting themselves. Obviously, they have come to a point of "knowing" (it's really *believing*) that God does not exist. Somehow, they have proved to themselves that this is the case. If they have proved it to themselves, then they should be able to prove it to me, but they can't, and they know they can't, so they rely on the "you can't prove a negative" ploy. All I'm asking is that they present to me what has caused them to believe what they believe.

It is truly pitiful that these individuals are not aware of the problems in their own belief system yet arrogantly attack my position. This is what people do to God all the time. Much of the non-Christian world believes that God does not exist. They have not seen Him, therefore He has given no real proof of His existence. Because of this, they believe that somehow "proves" that God does not exist.

The arrogance of human beings can be staggering! Imagine how much God sees and hears on a daily basis, yet He continues to ignore it for the time being in the hopes that these same people will come to the realization that their viewpoints about God are decidedly wrong. He wants them to see Him through the eyes of faith so that He might reward them with salvation. Is this too much to ask?

I've also noticed a trend in which many atheists are actually rising to the defense of Islam to an extent, telling me that Christianity is far worse because of all the evils that have been perpetrated in the Name of God. While I would agree that there have been many atrocities done in God's Name, this is by no means the fault of God *or* that of authentic Christians.

People like this do not want to hear about the wheat and the tares in which Jesus explains that Satan came along and sowed tares as soon as the Church was born (cf. Matthew 13:24-30; 36-43). Those tares will *never* be wheat, yet they often appear to *resemble* wheat. It is obvious that the world sees the tares as authentic wheat when it is clearly not the case.

In spite of all the teaching that Jesus provided on how badly His Church would be attacked, people seem not to care what He said because they are too intent on pulling down authentic Christians. They are so desperate to prove their case that they ignore even the most obvious signs of being wrong.

Yet in all of this God's patience prevails, for now. There will come a time when He will arrive at the end of His patience and put His judgments into action. Fortunately, that time is not now, and people still have the opportunity to turn to Him.

This is exactly the way the father in the parable treated his sons. He hoped that one day they would come to the realization that He was not the type of father they had come to believe he was, and he did what he could to engender that attitude within his sons.

Up until the time the younger son returned, nothing seemed to work. Yet the father continued to love his sons.

Luke 15:20
"But while he was still a long way off, his father saw him and felt compassion for him, and ran and embraced him and kissed him."

Who among us would do what the father did? While you might believe that you would do this, please think again, because it is likely that you do not really understand the import of the parable.

Human beings do not naturally set aside wrongs committed against them. It certainly should be done and can be done, but only with God's help.

This father's reputation had been trashed by his son. The son treated the father as if he was nothing and demanded what he had no right to demand. Yet his father gave the son what he wanted, hoping against hope that the young son would come to realize that he had not withheld anything, and even though societal norms would have been on the father's side had he chose to reject his son's demands, the father did what he could to *gain* his son's affections.

After the son lived his life of sin for a season, he returned to his waiting father. As was pointed out, it is clear that the father was looking for his son, probably glancing many times throughout each day to the horizon in the direction that his son had left. He hoped that one day he would see the silhouette of his son returning.

Then one day, it happened! Here was a figure, and from a distance it looked like it could be his son. Yes, it *was* his son, and the father wasted no time in looking like a fool by hiking up the folds of his robe and *running* toward his son!

When he reached his son, he knew from what his son said that the son had returned home with a new attitude. I'm not sure that this would have made a difference to the father. He was simply glad above all things that his son had returned.

It took the young son a great deal of money, lots of loose living, and falling to very low depths before he realized that he had it far better at home. The truth hit him and it hit him hard, and he *acted* on that truth. Instead of ignoring or rejecting it, he *embraced* it and did what was necessary to follow through on that truth. Because of it, he now saw his father in a completely different light.

Again, this represents just how far God went to gain our attention and fellowship! He sent His Son to die so that we might have access to Him.

In the parable, the father's love was constant and unwavering. He never faltered in his love for either of his sons. They faltered because they did not understand their father as he was and ascribed to him instead a personality that did not belong to him. In that way, they not only misunderstood their father but based their terrible decisions on their complete misunderstanding of him.

This is no different from what Adam and Eve or you and I do. We at times will come to see God as something He is not and because of that errant view, we make terrible decisions. What is worse, we wind up often bringing great harm to ourselves because of that erroneous view of God.

Jesus spent time trying to help the people see that God was not like the God the Pharisees described or taught about. Their lives did not reflect God's attitude. They were far off.

Jesus wanted them to know in no uncertain terms that God love them immensely and had done so many things to prove His love. This is how God is toward us as well. To us, He has an infinite amount of patience that stems from his immeasurable love.

We need to spend time in His Word and in communion with Him in order to come to know just exactly who God is and how He views us. God loves us and wants the best for us. That best starts with His salvation and grows from there.

Please notice that not once did the father in the parable ever try to make his sons feel guilty. He never used guilt cues or harsh language with them. The father in the parable was always gentle and fully loving. In fact, he was far more loving than his sons deserved. The same can be said with the way God responds to us.

When the son returned, he knew he had sinned. He knew he had brought dishonor to his father's household. The son knew that he had actually disgraced his father before neighbors and friends.

Yet when the son arrived home, not *once* did the father try to make his son feel as though he would have to earn his (the father's) respect. Not once is there even a *hint* of displeasure from the father to the son.

The son expected that his father *might* allow him to become a servant in his father's household. He certainly had not expected that his sins against his father and heaven would be forgiven so completely. He *never* expected to be embraced and kissed by his father, whom he had so terribly dishonored.

The father never made his son kneel before him and grovel. He did not give him the cold shoulder or ignore him altogether. The father did not treat his son as if he was a worm and would have nothing to do with him until the son realized just how bad he was and how evil were his actions.

No, the father did none of these things. Instead, the father pushed aside the sins of his son, forgetting them, never even *mentioning* them. The father embraced his son *as his son*, not a servant. The father treated his son as royalty, though the son would be the first to say that he did not deserve to be treated in such a way.

The father represents God. This is what Jesus is telling us. God will no sooner beat His children over the head with their sin than the father in the parable beat his son over the head with his sin.

The father in the parable knew that his son and *returned* and that he had done so by *walking away* from that sinful lifestyle. The father realized that for the son to have made this decision, he had come to understand exactly what he had done.

The son exhibited a far greater sense of maturity and understanding than did his older brother. By sinning and literally going off on his own and returning with a new and different attitude, the young son had learned just how much his father loved him. In fact, he likely began to realize that his father had *always* loved him like this, but he (the son) was too blind to see it because his eyes had always been on himself.

The young son was changed and he was changed forever. The older son was a different story altogether. He could not appreciate why the son had returned and what he had learned that caused him to return. All he saw was the young son's selfishness and how he dishonored the father.

The older son represents the legalism that was often displayed by the Pharisees and religious leaders. It is the legalism that exists today within the hearts of many people who call themselves Christians. Are they truly Christians? Certainly only God knows. One thing we can learn from them is that they have a very skewed understanding of God's love. They do not nor can they appreciate how much God loves us and how much He has deliberately forgotten about us where our sin is concerned.

The legalist cannot appreciate it because they do not believe that God has forgiven *them* their sin. They believe they must adopt this attitude and demeanor that sees God as a hard taskmaster, someone who expects much and gives little. This is not the God of the Bible as far as I can see. It is a god they have created so that SELF will remain firmly on the throne of their life. They have not learned what the young son learned: that God loves them, and every time we sin and *return* to Him by changing our direction and walking away from that sin (repentance), He waits with open arms, ready to embrace and kiss us.

The legalist cannot handle this type of God. It goes against their grain. To them, God cracks a whip and we need to "shape up."

This is *not* what the parable of the prodigal son tells us. It unfolds a far greater story about the truth of God's love and how much he desires to be in fellowship with us.

When we sin, God certainly does not participate in that at all. However, He waits diligently until we recognize that we *have* sinned, and when he sees us turning our face back to Him and turning our back on the sin, He *delights* in that!

God loves you. If you are His child, He has forgiven you. Since He has forgiven you, you are no longer condemned.

Chapter 9

No More Condemnation

"Therefore there is now no condemnation for those who are in Christ Jesus." – Romans 8:1

It is so difficult for us to imagine and comprehend. Paul tells us in Romans 8:1 that we are no longer condemned. If that is the case, then it is obvious that He has removed *all* of our sin, past, present, and future.

If His death did not eradicate and cancel our future sin, what was the point of His death, to simply cancel out *our past* sins? If you are a legalist, you are probably yelling, "YES!" I submit to you that His death cancels *all* of our sin. We are not living in the Old Testament times where the sacrifices that we brought before the Lord only *covered* (but did not *cancel*) our sin. We are living on this side of the cross, and because of that the purification for sins has been fully completed. This is extremely difficult for people to understand, and I will also admit that I'm still working through it.

On one hand, the Bible says we are no longer condemned. On the other hand, we still need to confess our sins as they occur. While that may seem like a contradiction, it really is not.

What we have learned so far in this book is that Jesus completed His work for redemption on the cross. We have also learned that as far as we are concerned, our lives – past, present, and future – are always before God. All of history from start to finish is always before God. This is extremely difficult for us to grasp, about as difficult as trying to define and understand the doctrine of the Trinity.

The Bible and especially the New Testament seems to speak to two sides of the same coin. On one side of the coin is our salvation, which I believe is secure and as good as fully accomplished. In Ephesians 2, Paul speaks of the fact that we have been raised with Christ. He says that in Jesus, we were *"raised...up with Him, and seated... with Him in the heavenly places in Christ Jesus"* (Ephesians 2:6). This is in our *past tense*, but God's present. In effect, because of the cross work of Jesus and our faith in that work, we receive salvation from God. Part of that salvation includes being raised to new life. This is now, even though we will never live it perfectly in this life.

We have been raised to new life and because of that we have that new life within us (through the indwelling Holy Spirit) to live apart from sin. At the same time, we continue to live with our sin nature, which will not be removed until we die. At this point an instantaneous spiritual surgery will be undertaken by Jesus, whereby our "old man" (the flesh, the sin nature) will be fully removed. From that point onward, we will fully live in the strength of the new man with nothing to interfere or cause us to sin.

In effect, these are done deals because they have already been accomplished. As far as God is concerned, we are already new and living without sin because when He sees us, He sees the righteousness of Jesus, which has been imputed to our accounts because of the new birth.

We talked about this in the first part of this book. Paul confirms these things for us in a number of places, but he brings it out firmly and coherently in Romans 8.

If we are no longer condemned, why are we condemning ourselves? By the way, I realize that certain translations state it this way: "*There is therefore now no condemnation to those who are in Christ Jesus, who do not walk according to the flesh, but according to the Spirit*" (NKJV).

Notice in that translation the phrase, "*who do not walk according to the flesh, but according to the Spirit.*" If you talk to people who are essentially KJV only people, they will tell you that this is the *correct* translation and other translations that leave this phrase out are fully *incorrect.*

But if we drop down a few more verses to verse four of Romans 8, we read this, "*that the righteous requirement of the law might be fulfilled in us who do not walk according to the flesh but according to the Spirit*" (NKJV).

Notice that the last part of that phrase is the exact same phrase that some translations include in verse one of Romans 8. In other words, not all manuscripts include that phrase after verse one of Romans 8. Some language experts believe that the inclusion of this phrase in the KJV is actually a scribal error that may have been listed in the margin and then simply added to the text later as if it was part of it.

If this phrase *is* part of the first verse, then it *can* change the meaning of it. People read it as I've quoted it from the NKJV and what they read is that those who *do not walk according to the flesh* are no longer condemned. If the phrase was never there in the first place, it is stating clearly that once a Christian receives salvation, he/she is no longer condemned at all. This understanding seems to square with the overall meaning of the New Testament far better than it does if the phrase is included.

The fact that this exact same phrase is included in verse four also tends to give credence to the belief that it was added to the margins by an over-zealous scribe at some point and then eventually became part of the translated text. I know KJV only people do not like to hear that because many of them believe that the KJV is as God-inspired as the original autographs written by God through human authors. I do not ascribe to that view.

Let me list the entire first few verses in two separate translations and see if we can see the difference in meaning. First, I'll quote from the NKJV, and then the NASB. Here is Romans 8:1-5:

"There is therefore now no condemnation to those who are in Christ Jesus, who do not walk according to the flesh, but according to the Spirit. For the law of the Spirit of life in Christ Jesus has made me free from the law of sin and death. For what the law could not do in that it was weak through the flesh, God did by sending His own Son in the likeness of sinful flesh, on account of sin: He condemned sin in the flesh, that the righteous requirement of the law might be fulfilled in us who do not walk according to the flesh but according to the Spirit. For those who live according to the flesh set their minds on the things of the flesh, but those who live according to the Spirit, the things of the Spirit."

"Therefore there is now no condemnation for those who are in Christ Jesus. For the law of the Spirit of life in Christ Jesus has set you free from the law of sin and of death. For what the Law could not do, weak as it was through the flesh, God did: sending His own Son in the likeness of sinful flesh and as an offering for sin, He condemned sin in the flesh, so that the requirement of the Law might be fulfilled in us, who do not

walk according to the flesh but according to the Spirit. For those who are according to the flesh set their minds on the things of the flesh, but those who are according to the Spirit, the things of the Spirit."

In the first translation, there is this definite sense that for me to no longer be condemned, I must walk according to the Spirit and not according to the flesh. Yet further down, the meaning with the exact same phrase is slightly different. While in the first verse it appears as though our condemnation or lack of it is dependent upon what we do and how we live, in the verses further down, it appears to say that we *are* walking according to the Spirit because God's Spirit lives within us.

It is clear that in both translations, Paul is saying that we are truly free from the law of sin and death. How did that happen? Jesus did it. Paul says that following the Law could not do this at all, and in fact, the Law only destroyed by pointing out every time I sinned. Sin leads to death; therefore, to live under the constraints of the Law with my sin nature ultimately means that I will die eternally.

But God sent God the Son, Jesus, to do what I could not do in my flesh, and that is to walk according to the Spirit. I am only capable of walking according to the Law. Jesus fulfilled the demands and dictates of the Law because I am simply unable to do that, no ifs, ands, or buts. The reality is that since I could not keep the Law, I was dead. Jesus fulfilled it *for me* so that I was free to receive His salvation. Once I received His salvation I became a completely new creature.

Doesn't Paul say this in 2 Corinthians 5:17? *"Therefore if anyone is in Christ, he is a new creature; the old things passed away; behold, new things have come."* Certainly appears that way, and it ties in with Romans 8 rather nicely because Paul is talking about the same thing, isn't he?

Paul says that *if* I am *in* Christ, I am a new creature. What does Paul mean when he uses the term "in" Christ? It means I have received salvation and have been baptized *into* the Body of Christ, the true Church.

So when Paul speaks of our walking according to the Spirit, he is saying that overall, we will do this *because* we are in Christ, not *if* we are in Christ. Paul is not saying that it is questionable whether or not we are in Christ. His use of the term "if" simply means that if a person *is an authentic Christian*, they are walking according to the Spirit.

Many people who disagree with this believe that the Holy Spirit exercises no authority over the believer and will not chastise or work within that believer to make him/her into a new creature. These people think that the oneness is on the Christian. While yes, we have a role to play, that role is solely found in *submitting* ourselves to God.

For instance, if I am at my computer and one of those stupid pop-up ads comes up with a scantily-clad woman on it, I have a choice. I can ignore it by closing it, or I can click on it and follow the link to the site where I may likely see more scantily-clad women (or worse!). My choice is simple. Do I submit myself to the Lord or do I cave in to the demands of the flesh? Because I have the sin nature, which is alive and well within me, I will either be submitting myself to God by *ignoring* the demands and temptations of the sin nature, or I will be submitting myself to the *sin nature*, ignoring the fact that I am *in Christ*.

If I wind up submitting myself to the dictates of my sinful nature, I will be harming my fellowship with God, but I do not lose my salvation, nor do I receive God's *condemnation*. Remember, my future sins have also been forgiven. This does *not* mean that I am free to do whatever I want whether it pleases God or not. We dealt with this in an earlier section of this book. We are *never* free to live the life of a non-Christian once we become part of the Lord's Body.

At the same time, I know that I *will* from time to time *sin,* and it is not something that I *really* want to do.

Paul speaks of this problem in Romans as well. He tells us about this struggle in Romans 7.

"For we know that the Law is spiritual, but I am of flesh, sold into bondage to sin. For what I am doing, I do not understand; for I am not practicing what I would like to do, but I am doing the very thing I hate. But if I do the very thing I do not want to do, I agree with the Law, confessing that the Law is good. So now, no longer am I the one doing it, but sin which dwells in me. For I know that nothing good dwells in me, that is, in my flesh; for the willing is present in me, but the doing of the good is not. For the good that I want, I do not do, but I practice the very evil that I do not want. But if I am doing the very thing I do not want, I am no longer the one doing it, but sin which dwells in me.

"I find then the principle that evil is present in me, the one who wants to do good. For I joyfully concur with the law of God in the inner man, but I see a different law in the members of my body, waging war against the law of my mind and making me a prisoner of the law of sin which is in my members. Wretched man that I am! Who will set me free from the body of this death? Thanks be to God through Jesus Christ our Lord! So then, on the one hand I myself with my mind am serving the law of God, but on the other, with my flesh the law of sin." (Romans 7:14-25)

Without taking up a great deal of space to explain what Paul is saying (and I know various commentators interpret Paul's words differently), suffice it to say that I believe Paul is speaking of the ongoing struggle that takes place within the authentic Christian. Note how Paul says that he does the things he does not want to do and finds it difficult to do the things he knows he *should* do. This is a perfect picture of the authentic Christian's struggle against the sin nature we still possess even *after* we have become saved.

Christians do *not* become perfect when we accept Jesus. I know of people who actually believe that after Paul was saved, God removed his sin nature, and from that point onward Paul lived a sinless life. They say that this description Paul is giving is *before* he became a Christian compared with *after* he became one.

I personally think it is ridiculous to believe that God would make this special exemption for Paul. There was no need to do this at all. Jesus was the only individual who did not have a sin nature, and had He had one that alone would have disqualified Him to become the propitiation for our sin.

While Jesus was tempted in all ways that we are tempted, He was like Adam and Eve *before* they sinned and *before* they developed the sin nature as a result of their sin. Jesus is the only Man (though fully God) who *never* used *His* absolute free will to *rebel* against God the Father.

Satan had absolute free will prior to his fall, and he chose to use it for rebellious purposes. Both Adam and Eve had absolute free will and also chose to use it to rebel against the Lord. The sense is that creatures who are given absolute free will find it difficult to live under the authority of another. It begins to chafe, and therefore it is not long before sin is accomplished by listening to the dictates of that free will.

Jesus had absolute free will and yet never once gave into the constant pressure and temptation to use it to rebel against His Father. He always submitted Himself perfectly to every request and expectation of the Father. In that way, He perfectly fulfilled the entirety of the

Law, every jot and tittle, and because of it was found worthy to offer Himself as the sacrifice for our sins.

Jesus was the *only* One who lived a perfect, sinless life. We will *never* be able to do that as long as the sin nature remains with us. Paul's description of what life is like, having to live with something that constantly wants to pull us away from God and yet wanting to submit ourselves to God, is truly our lot in this life, even *after* we become Christians.

If you'll notice in the last few verses of the text I quoted from Romans 7, Paul asks the question, "*Who will set me free from this body of death? Thanks be to God through Jesus Christ our Lord! So then, on the one hand I myself with my mind* **am serving the law of God**, *but on the other,* **with my flesh the law of sin**" (emphasis added).

The truth is that this is a paradox that is difficult for us to fully appreciate. Paul is telling us that two things are at work within us. One is our newly created *mind* that fully desires to serve God in all things (serving the law of God), and yet the flesh (the sin nature or old man) also remains alive, constantly taunting and tempting us to give into the demands of the flesh, which is governed by the law of sin.

Paul is *not* saying that the Law is sinful or bad! He is saying that the Law constantly points out *our sin* because that is what it was designed to do. Had it not been for the law, we would not even have been aware that we *have* sinned by breaking it. The Law shows us unequivocally that we are sinners. It literally sells us into bondage, as Paul noted in Romans 7:1. We are slaves to the Law that brings forth death.

Once we become Christians, that bondage is broken. It does not mean that we will *never* sin. It means that we will continue to be *tempted* to sin, but we do not have to submit ourselves to that. We can instead submit ourselves to God because *He has freed us from the Law of death.* Because of this, we walk in the Spirit.

I'm not trying to minimize sin here, but when we sin, we trip and stumble. We need to recognize that we have fallen, confess it to God, get up and keep moving. If we fall down, stay down, and wallow in self-hatred, we are accomplishing nothing.

Imagine the runner who is running the race and trips. Does he/she stay down? No, a professional runner will get up quickly and try to make up the difference, still trying to win the race. They don't give up because they fell. They might get a bit frustrated or even possibly angry with themselves, but professional athletes *learn* from their mistakes. They don't curl up into a fetal position and berate themselves because they tripped over a rock they didn't see and fell.

If we continually condemn ourselves every time we fall, we are wasting valuable time and effort. We have allowed the enemy to focus our eyes on US. We have taken our eyes off the prize. While some think this is actually *spiritual*, it is the opposite of it. It actually winds up being self-aggrandizing without intending to be.

This is such a difficult topic, and I wish I understood it better than I do; more than that, I wish I could *explain* it better than I am doing. At the same time, if people are going to misrepresent Paul's words and he was a brilliant, learned individual, how can my words stand up to that same type of scrutiny?

I do *not* believe that God wants us to condemn ourselves. I do not believe that He wants or expects us to stay on the ground cursing ourselves because of our mistakes.

But Fred, someone might say, what about those Christians who fall *seriously*? You mean the ones who commit adultery, or rape, or worse? The worse the offense (humanly speaking) the more seriously we should take it. I have to wonder, though, how a person could rape someone and claim to be Christian. How could someone live a life of adultery or hop from one bed to another and claim that they know the Lord?

I realize, of course, that people fall, and they will fall according to their own individual weaknesses. However, people usually do not fall by committing adultery. They actually *work up to that point* by first flirting with someone they might find attractive. Once they see that they have not "crossed the line" (in their mind), they might push it a bit further. Eventually, if they leave things unchecked, they will wind up in an adulterous affair because they fell quite some time ago, refused to acknowledge it and just plowed ahead.

In those cases where someone is truly a Christian, there are *societal* consequences that must come to play out on that situation. If a person was a pastor who committed adultery, he should step down and never go into formal pastoring again. He has disqualified himself from being a minister over people. He cannot be trusted to not succumb to that same problem in the future.

There have been many pastors who have given into this type of temptation and have been thrown out of the pastorate because of it. Some, however, refused to go and remained in the pulpit. Their level of effectiveness has been severely curtailed and their lack of humility has only made the situation worse.

We need only look to King David to see his failure, which started not with lust but with *laziness*. In 2 Samuel 11:1, we read these words (emphasis added): *"In the spring, at the time when kings go off to war, David sent Joab out with the king's men and the whole Israelite army. They destroyed the Ammonites and besieged Rabbah.* **But David remained in Jerusalem***."*

That was David's very first mistake. He *should* have been out actually leading his troops but instead decided he didn't want to do that. He preferred to remain in the luxury of his palace. Because of that, he grew bored and spent some time on his rooftop at night. It was not long before he saw a beautiful woman named Bathsheba bathing. While he *accidentally* saw her there, he *deliberately* kept looking. This, of course, simply heated up his lust, and before he knew it he had summoned her and slept with her! As if this was not bad enough, he then tried to cover his sin, but when that did not work he actually had her husband, Uriah, killed in battle. There, that took care of that! Not so, because God saw everything. Duh.

From that point onward, the sword never left David's house. His sinful actions tore his household apart and he forever lived to regret his stupidity and callousness.

Had he gone with his troops in the first place, he never would have been home to see Bathsheba nude. He never would have lusted after her and he never would have given into that lust. Ultimately, he never would have killed her husband.

King David was a *servant* of God! How could this happen? For one thing, the Holy Spirit *never* lived within anyone in the Old Testament. The most the Holy Spirit did was to come *upon* a person for a specific task, and when that task was completed, He normally went away. It was very difficult to be a godly person in those days. This is why the Law and the sacrificial system were so important.

Today, Christians have the privilege and constant benefit of the indwelling Holy Spirit. He will not leave us or forsake us. He is always within, helping us even when we are not aware of His presence and even when we don't think we need help.

It is far easier to live the Christian life on *this* side of the cross than it was on David's side of it. The indwelling Spirit provides us with strength, directs our steps, chastises us when we need it and always does everything in order to build us up and create within us the image of God the Son. This was *not* the case in the Old Testament.

You and I can think of many well-known TV evangelists who fell from grace because of one thing or another. Were they – *are* they – true Christians? I cannot judge their heart, but I can certainly judge their fruit, and you can too. In too many cases, it seems to be quite a racket they have for themselves, driving the most expensive cars, wearing the best clothing, owning the large homes on huge estates. How can this be? Is *this* why they have a ministry?

How can people be so seemingly duplicitous? How can they *say* they serve God but what we see seems to prove otherwise? Either these people are Christians or they are not.

All Christians sin from time to time. Every authentic Christian living today has and will make mistakes. The question, though, is whether they are living a *lifestyle* of sin or whether their sin happens only from time to time. All sin is wrong of course, but there *is* a huge difference between a lifestyle of sin and sinning occasionally.

God wants us to realize that we *are free* and that we do not have to follow the dictates of sin. We can successfully ignore it with God's indwelt strength.

Here's the problem, though. Not only does Satan want us to fall through sin, but he wants to condemn us when we are down. If we listen to him and sin, then we have sinned. If we continue to listen to his condemnation of us, we have sinned *again*.

Paul tells us in Romans 8:1 that we are no longer condemned because as far as God is concerned, we are walking in the Spirit. During those times when we fall down, we need to confess our failure to God, get up quickly, and keep moving! We cannot afford to wallow in our sin. We dare not take the time to make more of a stink about it than God does. Remember the prodigal son's father upon the young man's return?

Romans 8 closes with two or three verses that are just as valuable and eye-opening as the first verse. Let me quote them here. *"But in all these things we overwhelmingly conquer through Him who loved us. For I am convinced that neither death, nor life, nor angels, nor principalities, nor things present, nor things to come, nor powers, nor height, nor depth, nor any other created thing, will be able to separate us from the love of God, which is in Christ Jesus our Lord."* (Romans 8:37-39)

Please, *read that again.* Do you see what Paul is saying? He is saying that *nothing* – not one thing – can separate us from God's love. This includes our *sin* because it has already been dealt with at Calvary.

Our sin – *past, present, and future* – is *gone.* God no longer remembers it. It has been *cancelled* because of the blessing we have received through the finished work of Jesus.

If God no longer remembers our sin, why do you want to harp on it? Why do you want to spend time convincing yourself that you are worthless, a worm, a true sinner indeed?

Again, we should *never* make light of our sin. God does *not* want us to do to ourselves what He will *not* do. He will *never* condemn us, He will *always* love us, and there is *nothing* that can ever separate us from His love.

How is this cheap grace? It was very costly, and the more we submit ourselves to God, the more we will become like the prodigal son who returned to realize just how much his father loved him. It was that *love* that he experienced and received from his father that created within him the desire to *serve* his father. Oh, I'm sure that same young man made mistakes from time to time after he returned. Do you think for a moment that his father *condemned* him for them?

This same father who would *not* allow his son to even entertain the idea that he would not be considered his son anymore was the same father who loved his son with a seemingly endless love.

I fully believe that we do a tremendous disservice to God when we teach and believe that we must be extremely hard on ourselves when we sin. I believe this is not only counter-productive, but it denies the finished work of Jesus Christ.

If I condemn myself for my sins – any of them – I am focusing on sin itself. This is what the prodigal son wanted to do. He wanted to be nothing more than a servant in his father's house. How could he expect his father to receive him back as a son? That would be absurd.

The son's newfound humility told him that he was not worthy, and that much was certainly true. However, when he saw how much his father loved him and realized that there was not a question of whether or not he was forgiven, he began to understand the love that his father had for him, and it was because of this love that he knew he never wanted to *deliberately* and *purposefully* hurt his father again. Meanwhile, the older son simply wanted to *accuse*. This is exactly what Satan does with us, *accuses*.

Please notice that the prodigal son did *not* take his sin lightly. He understood it for what it was and realized that for all intents and purposes he could not expect his father to ever embrace him as a son again.

The son was extremely surprised when he reached home to realize that not only were his sins forgiven, but he was *still* his father's son! The prodigal son fully realized just how badly he had treated his father, and he was ready to pay the price for his sin. The father set the son's sin aside, continuing to treat him as a member of his family.

God loves us. He loves *you*. He does *not* want you to wallow in self-destructive hatred because of your failures. All that will do is cause *more* and *greater* failures! Get your mind off of your sin once you have confessed it and admitted to God that you *did* sin. Once you confess it, understand that God's reaction to you is exactly the same as the father's reaction to the prodigal son. Why do we try to make it *so* difficult? God is there for us. If you are His child, He is not now nor ever will condemn you.

Depending upon your sin, there may be societal repercussions that result from it (just as they occurred with David), but God will *not* condemn you. Moreover, Paul clearly tells us that there is nothing that we can do or nothing that can come against us that will separate us from His love for us.

Knowing this, you have two choices (and I am talking to authentic Christians now):

1. You can be extremely happy that you are forgiven and run off and live your life any way you choose, but don't expect God to sit back and let you do it!
2. You can also come to see and appreciate just exactly what God in Christ gave up for you.

If you opt for the first choice, please know that your life from that point onward will be *miserable*. Why? Because God will do what it takes to bring you back into fellowship with Him. If you find that you can live your life any way that you want to and never feel bad about how you are living your life, then I would submit to you that you do not know Him in the first place.

If you opt for the second choice, you will very likely draw closer to God each time you submit your life, your dreams, your hopes, and your wants to Him. In that case, your life will be blessed beyond measure as you come to know Him better each day. You will notice that your attitude will change and that you will actually come to the point where you *want* to submit your life to Him so that He can work in and through you. Not being in communion with Him is not something you want to happen because you have grown to love Him so much for what He has done for you.

There is only one way to live the Christian life, and it is by voluntarily submitting your life to God. We can try to "kick against the goads," as it were, but we will wind up simply hurting ourselves because God will have His way.

If you are one of His children, having received the only salvation that is available to you through Jesus, God has fully *forgiven* you. He no longer *condemns* you and nothing can *separate* you from His love. These truths are very difficult for us to believe, aren't they? We are still buying into the false notion that we have to work to *please* God. When we fail to work, we are in danger of losing our salvation.

This is not what God's Word tells me. The grace that extends from God to His own is *not* cheap. It does *not* give us a license to sin. True grace, rightly understood, grants us the ability to submit ourselves to God for His good pleasure.

What could be better? What could be more beneficial? What could bless us more? Nothing. Nothing at all. There is nothing better than God's love as seen in the grace He extends to us.

It is that grace that draws us to Him, and it is that grace that *keeps* us bound to Him. We will fall short from time to time, but He is always there to catch us, to help us up, and to brush us off. He understands the constraints we live under, with the ever-present sin nature constantly vying for attention and for top position in our lives.

It is this wonderful grace that allows us to understand that God no longer condemns us and that nothing that we do will ever separate us from His love. As the father in the parable of the prodigal son never stopped loving his son and never condemned him upon his return to his father, how much *more* is God the Father like that to us?

It is beyond measure. Please, stop condemning yourself when you fail, because He no longer condemns you. When you sin, confess it; agree with Him that you *did* sin and you are truly sorry for it. Confess it, forget it, and move on. Remember He is holding your hand, and if necessary, He will carry you.

His grace extends to the darkest places in our mind and heart. There is nothing hidden from Him, so we need to stop pretending as if there is, and we need to realize that His love is greater than any sin we could commit...except the sin of *unbelief.* Start believing God when He says He no longer condemns you. Take Him at His Word when He tells you that nothing can separate us from His love.

To do anything else is to not believe Him.

Chapter 10

The End

"For all have sinned, and come short of the glory of God." – Romans 3:23

D o you know *when* you will die? Are you aware of the *day* and *hour* when you will slip from this life into eternity? I'm betting you are not privy to that information. So why are you living as if you **do** *know when it will happen?* Putting a decision about Jesus off until another day is taking a huge chance because of the fact that you do not know when you will die. That is plainly simple, and logic alone demands that you do not put this decision off. Yet you do, because the thought of becoming a Christian makes you feel uncomfortable.

You wrongly believe that to become a Christian means that you have to change in a major way *before* Jesus will accept you. It means to you giving up the things you love now because if you love them, then obviously they are wrong and God does not love them.

You are putting the cart before the horse. You must understand that God is not rejecting you. He is not standing there, tapping His foot, demanding that you eliminate those things that He does not like before you can come to Him for salvation.

If you (or anyone) could do that, you would not *need* His salvation at all. It is because you and I do things that are not pleasing to Him that we need His salvation.

What do you do that you would like to no longer do? Do you drink excessively until you cannot control it? Do you play around with drugs? Do you eat too much food until you have become overweight, lethargic and sickly?

What other things are in your life that you do not like? Are you drawn to illicit extra-marital affairs? Do you have a problem with lust? Are you a shopaholic? Do you tend to tell lies a great deal because it makes you feel important, or to hide things about your life?

Do you find that you do not like people and you would prefer to be around animals or out in the woods than around people? Are you a workaholic? Do you place a high value on money and you find that you work very hard to obtain it?

Here's the problem. The enemy of our souls comes to us and tells us that God will never accept us until we get rid of those things. He lies to us that God essentially wants us "perfect" before He will be willing to meet us and grant us eternal life. This is completely untrue.

The other lie that our enemy tells us is that we should not become a Christian because the fun in our life will fly out the door. We will no longer be able to drink or do the fun things we enjoy now. We start to think that coming to God means becoming a doormat for people and having to fill our life with things we do not want to *ever* do.

These are all lies, and unfortunately, too many people believe them. First of all, God does not expect you to be "perfect" before you come to Him for salvation. If that were the case, no one would be able to ever approach Him.

Secondly, God does not say that He is going to take away all the things we enjoy and replace them with things we hate. What is wrong with enjoying the lake on your boat? What is wrong with spending a day with the family fishing or just relaxing in the mountains? There is nothing wrong with these things.

What God *will* do is begin to remove the things that have ensnared you so that life is actually draining from you, but you are not aware of it. For instance, maybe you drink excessively and you have tried everything you can think of to quit. You have gone to AA meetings, spent thousands of dollars on this program or that, and you have even used your own will power to free yourself from the addiction to alcohol, all to no avail.

The question is not: *do I need to quit before I come to Jesus*? The question is: *am I willing to allow Him to work in and through me to take away the addiction I have to alcohol*? Do you see the difference? Are you willing to allow Him to work in you to break that addiction so that you will become a healthier person, one who is able to think straight and one who learns to rely on Him for strength? That is all He wants you to be able to do. He knows you cannot break that addiction (or any addiction for that matter) with your own strength and willpower. Are you willing to allow Him to do it in and through you?

What if you are a workaholic? What if you have "things" like a boat, a house in Cancun, a large bank account, four cars, and more? Do you think that God is going to ask you to give it up, or worse, do you think that God will simply come in and take all of that from you? I know of nothing in Scripture that tells us He will do that.

What God will do with all of those who come to Him trusting Him for salvation is one thing, which begins the moment we receive salvation and will continue until the day we stand before Him. He will begin to create within us the character of Jesus (cf. Ephesians 2:10).

Here is a verse from the Old Testament that was said originally through the prophet Ezekiel to the people of Israel. While this was specifically stated to the Jews, it is applicable to all who receive salvation through Jesus Christ.

"I will give you a new heart and put a new spirit within you; I will take the heart of stone out of your flesh and give you a heart of flesh. I will put My Spirit within you and cause you to walk in My statutes, and you will keep My judgments and do them" (Ezekiel 36:26-27).

God is speaking here through Ezekiel, and He is saying that He will give the people a new heart of flesh, removing that old heart of stone. This is God's responsibility. God is the One who makes that happen. We are told in the book of Hebrews that God is the Author and Finisher of our faith (cf. Hebrews 12:2). This tells me that God is the One who changes me from within so that over time, my desires are slowly turned into His desires.

I recall years ago thinking that God wanted to do everything in my life that I did not want Him to do. I fell into the asinine belief that He wanted to change everything about me. What I learned is that yes, there are things that God does want to change about me. However, there is a lot that God originally gave me that He has also enhanced and used for His glory.

Maybe you are a workaholic who thinks that working hard is something God does not want you to do. This is not necessarily the case. He may have given you the ability and the knowledge to work in the area of finance for a great purpose. All He may wind up doing is dialing back your workaholic tendencies so that you have more time to enjoy your family and study His Word.

But you say you smoke, or drink, or use illegal drugs, and you don't want to give those up. As I stated, you can't give those up under your own power, and the fact that you have tried so many times has proven it to you.

But God knows what is and what is not good for you. Are you willing to *allow* Him to work in you to change your desires so that you no longer want to smoke, use illegal drugs, or drink nearly as much?

Then you say that you believe God wants to make you a Christian so you can become miserable. Isn't that what most Christians are – miserable? Not the Christians I know, and certainly not me, my wife, or our children.

Where does the Bible say that God wants us miserable? You will not find it. What God wants is for us to be blessed, and that begins when we receive salvation from His hand.

You know, if we would stop and take the time to consider the fact that this life is exceedingly short if we compare it to eternity, we will then realize that there is nothing so important that it should keep us from receiving Jesus as Savior and Lord.

Unfortunately, too many people do not consider the brevity of life. They think they will live forever, or at the very least, they will die when they are really old and gray. That will come too soon. Even though I have just recently turned 54, it still truly seems like yesterday that I was a young boy fishing in the Delaware River near Hobart, New York. There I spent many Saturdays fishing and simply enjoying being outdoors. How did life go by so very quickly? How could that have happened?

It has happened, and I am at a point in life where not only do I realize that this life is short, but I actually look forward to spending eternity with Jesus after this life. Does that sound morbid to you? It shouldn't, because by comparing this life to eternity, we should get a sense of what is truly important.

God does not expect us to become Mother Theresas. He does not necessarily expect us to give up everything and become missionaries in outer Mongolia. What God expects is for us to simply allow Him to change our character as He sees fit.

Over time, we may well find that we have simply stopped swearing without realizing it. Our desire for cigarettes or alcohol has nearly evaporated. Illicit affairs no longer enter the picture.

We also may find that some of the things we want to eliminate in our life become more pronounced. Often the enemy will do this to cause us to focus on something that God is not even doing in our lives at that point. It causes tension, frustration, and self-anger.

If you have gotten to this point in your life and you have not dealt with the question about Jesus, it is about time you do so. You need to stop what you are doing and realize a couple of things before you go through another minute in this life.

- **Sinner**: you need to realize that you are a sinner. You have sinned and you will continue to sin. Sin is breaking the laws that God has set up. We all sin. We have all broken God's laws and that breaks any connection we might have had with God.

Sin pushes us away from Him.

Romans 3:23 says, *"For all have sinned, and come short of the glory of God."* That means you and that means me. All means all. That is the first step. We need to recognize and agree with God that yes, we are sinners. I'm a sinner. You are a sinner. This results in God's anger, what the Bible terms "wrath."

- **God's Wrath**: Romans 1:18 says, *"For the wrath of God is revealed from heaven against all ungodliness and unrighteousness of men, who suppress the truth in unrighteousness."*

This is as much a fact as the truth that we are all sinners. Because we are sinners – by breaking God's law(s) – God has every right to be angry with us and ultimately destroy that which is sinful. If we choose to remain "in" our sinful states throughout this life, we will – unfortunately – be destroyed with the rest of sin.

Fortunately, there *is* a remedy, and it is salvation.

- **God's Gift**: In the sixteenth chapter of Acts, a jailer asks Paul this famous question: *what must I do to be saved?* The question was asked because Paul and Barnabas had been imprisoned, and while there, they began singing praises to God.

God then sent a powerful earthquake that opened the doors to all the prison cells, yet no one escaped. When the jailer arrived, he saw that everyone was still in their cells, and after seeing that miracle (what prisoner would not want to escape from prison?), turned and asked what he must do to be saved. He was speaking of the spiritual aspect of things. He wanted to know how he could be guaranteed eternal life.

The answer Paul gave the man was, "*Believe on the Lord Jesus Christ, and thou shalt be saved, and thy house*" (Acts 16:31).

This is not head knowledge or intellectual assent. This is *believing from the heart.* In fact, Paul makes a very similar statement in another book he wrote, Romans. He says, "*That if thou shalt confess with thy mouth the Lord Jesus, and shalt believe in thine heart that God hath raised him from the dead, thou shalt be saved. For with the heart man believeth unto righteousness; and with the mouth confession is made unto salvation*" (Romans 10:9-10).

When we fully believe something, we confess that it is true. It must begin in the heart because that is where the will is located. We must want to believe. We must endeavor to believe. We must seek to believe.

We must stop giving ourselves all the reasons to deny or ignore Jesus. As God, He became a Man, born of a virgin. He clothed Himself with humanity that He might show us how to live, and in so doing, would keep every portion of the law.

If Jesus was capable of keeping every portion of the law, then He would be found worthy to become a sacrifice for our sin – yours and mine. If He became a sacrifice for our sin, then all that we must do is embrace Him and His sacrificial death.

In short then, to become saved we must:

1. Admit (we sin)

2. Repent (want to turn away from it)
3. Believe (that Jesus is the answer)
4. Embrace (the truth about Jesus)

We **admit** that we are sinner, that we have sinned. This is nothing more than agreeing with God that we have broken His law. Can you honestly say that you have not broken God's law? If you admit to breaking even the "smallest" law, then you are a lawbreaker.

After we admit that we have sinned, the next step is found in **repenting**. Some believe that repenting is actually moving away from sin. This author believes that it is a willingness to move away from sin, and there is a difference.

As we have already discussed, it is impossible to stop sinning. Human beings simply cannot do it because as long as we live, we will have a sin nature, which is something within us that gives us a propensity to sin. As long as we have this inner propensity to sin or break God's laws, we will never be perfect in this life.

We cannot one day say, "Lord, I promise to stop sinning." If we do that, we are only kidding ourselves and setting ourselves up for major failure. We cannot stop sinning in this life. The most we can do is *want* to stop sinning and then spend the rest of our lives allowing God to create the character of Jesus within us, slowly, little by little.

Repenting is to decide that you no longer want to do the things that keep us out of heaven. We no longer wish to break God's laws. It is not promising God that we will never sin again.

Once we admit, then repent, we must **believe**. This is one of the most difficult things to do because believing that Jesus died in our place, that He lived a perfectly sinless life, is extremely difficult to believe. Our minds cannot grasp that truth. We must ask God to open our eyes to that truth so that we can embrace it.

While on the cross next to Jesus, the one thief joined the other thief in ridiculing Jesus. Then, all of a sudden – as we read in Luke 23 – this same thief that had just been ridiculing Him now turned to Him with a new understanding.

It was this new understanding that prompted the thief to say to Jesus, *"Lord, remember me when you come into your Kingdom."* Jesus looked at the man and responded to him, *"Today, you will be with me in paradise."*

What had occurred in the mind and heart of that thief from one moment to the next? One thing, and that one thing was that God opened the thief's eyes so that he could see the truth. It was as if the blinders fell off and he now saw and understood who Jesus was, even to the most cursory degree that Jesus was dying not for Himself, but for others.

It was this understanding, this awareness, which prompted the man to ask Jesus to simply be remembered. Jesus went way beyond it to promise the man that he would be with Jesus that day in paradise.

Please notice in Luke 23 that there is nothing in the chapter that tells us that the man promised Jesus he would give up sin, or that he would never sin again. There is nothing that tells us that thief took the time to enter into a final deathbed confession of his sins so that he could be absolved.

The thief made no promises to Jesus at all. What he experienced was the truth of who Jesus was and what Jesus accomplished for humanity. Jesus accomplished what we cannot. What is left is for each person to *admit, repent, believe,* and *embrace.*

Let me clarify here that though we do not see any verbal repentance from the thief, we know that he did repent. He admitted as well. How can we know this? Simply due to the thief's complete about-face with respect to his attitude toward Jesus. One minute, he was ridiculing Jesus, and the next, embracing Him. This is important. There is no way he could have or would have *embraced* Jesus had he not been humbled by the truth *about* Jesus.

Once the thief saw the truth, he was instantly humbled. Within himself, he knew that he was a sinner, and in fact the text states that this is what he told the other thief dying next to him. *"But the other answering rebuked him, saying, Dost not thou fear God, seeing thou art in the same condemnation? And we indeed justly; for we receive the due reward of our deeds: but this man hath done nothing amiss"* (Luke 23:40-41). Something happened within the heart of the one thief. In one moment, the thief went from harassing Jesus to recognizing his own sinfulness and then ultimately asking for grace, which was freely given to him.

Whether he said it or not, the thief went from haughtiness to humility in a very short space of time, and it was all because he saw the truth about Jesus. That truth helped him realize that he deserved his death and what would happen to him after death. He understood that Jesus did not deserve death.

From here, the thief fully embraced the truth about Jesus and was rewarded with eternal life because of it. He did not come off the cross to be water baptized. He did not list a long litany of offenses against God. He recognized the truth about Jesus, was humbled, and embraced that truth!

This is what each of us needs to do. We cannot give in to the lie that tells us that we are not good enough, or we have not given up enough before God will accept us. We must reject the lie that says we must somehow earn our salvation.

Jesus has done everything that is necessary to make salvation available to us. The only thing that is left for us is to see the truth.

Once we see that truth, it should humble us to the point of embracing Jesus and all that He stands for and is to us.

The eighth chapter of Romans begins with the fact that all who trust Jesus for salvation are no longer condemned...*ever*. All of my sins – past, present, and future – have not only been forgiven, but canceled. It is because of my faith in the atonement (death) of Jesus that God is able to cancel all of my sins, even the ones that I have not committed yet. This does not make me eager to commit them. It makes me want to do what I can to avoid sinning.

If you do not know Jesus, please do not put down this book without deliberately *believing* that He is God, that He died for you by the shedding of His blood on the cross, and that He rose three days later because death could not keep Him. Do you believe that? If you do not yet believe it, do you *want* to believe it? If so, then simply ask God to help you come to believe all that Jesus is and all that He has accomplished for you. God will answer your prayers and you may either receive instantaneous awareness of all that Jesus is and has done, or it may be a *growing* awareness over time. In either case, it is the most important decision you will ever make.

Turn to Him now and pray for knowledge of the truth and an ability to embrace it. Please. He is waiting for you.

Ask Yourself:

1. Do you *know* Jesus? Are you in *relationship* with Him? Have you had a spiritual transaction according to John 3?
2. Do you *want* to receive eternal life through the only salvation that is available?
3. Do you believe that Jesus is God the Son, who was born of a virgin, lived a sinless life, died a bloody and gruesome death to pay for your sin, was buried, and rose again on the third day? Do you *believe* this?
4. Do you *want* to *embrace* the truth from #3?

5. Pray that God will open your eyes and provide you with the faith to begin believing the truth about Jesus. Ask Him to help your faith embrace the truth, realizing that you are not good enough to save yourself and that your sin will keep you out of God's Kingdom without His salvation.
6. Pray as if your life depended upon it because *it does*!
7. If you have prayed to receive Jesus as Savior and Lord, please write to me. I want to send you some materials at *no charge or obligation*. Write to me at **fred_deruvo@hotmail.com** and sign up for our free bimonthly newsletter at **www.studygrowknow.com**

Visit our page on **OnePlace.com/ministries/study-grow-know** to hear our latest broadcasts as well as those that have been archived.

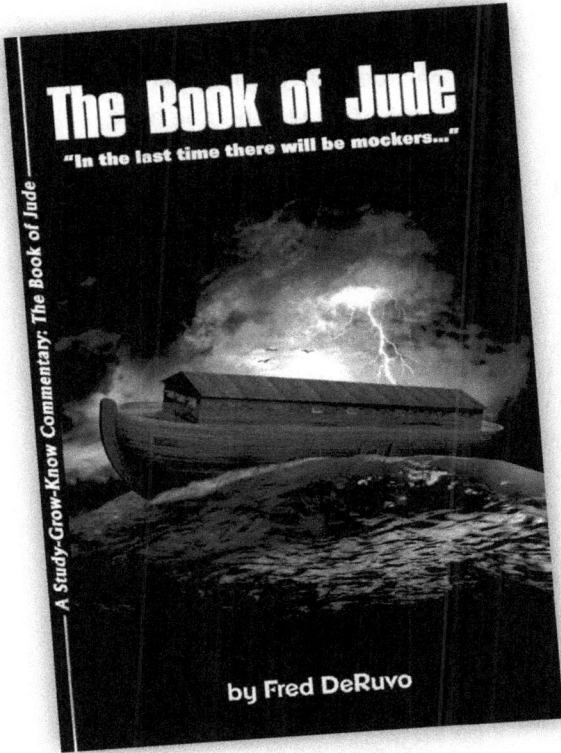

The book of Jude is only twenty-five verses in length, but it packs a spiritual wallop! Jude, the brother of James (and half-brother of our Lord Jesus), writes a message to believers about the times in which they lived. Those times are not at all that much different from the days in which we now live. Jude warns against apostasy, licentiousness, and the mockers that are destined to be part of the last days. Even during Jude's day, mocking the Lord's return had already begun. How much worse is it today, roughly 2,000 years later? ($11.99; 126 pages, 978-0983700692)

Everyone has an opinion. It does not matter whether you're a New Ager, a UFO researcher, a student of the Bible, or simply a curious party. Theories regarding aliens range from believing that the whole alien phenomenon is nothing more than an elaborate hoax, to the belief that they are real and getting ready to take over our world, to the view that they are demons disguising themselves as aliens.

($15.99; 206 pages, 978-0982644393)

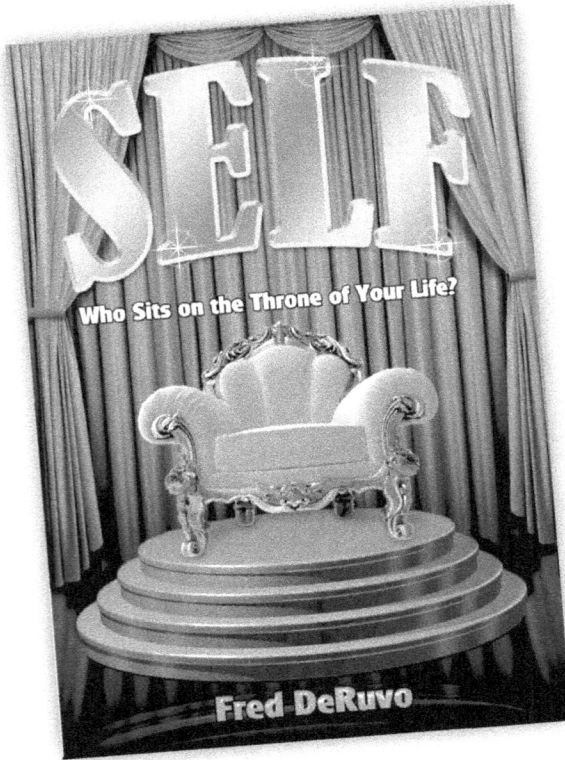

Society has changed drastically over the past decades. Why is that? Simply due to the fact that people have become more preoccupied with *Self*. In this book, Dr. Fred presents *Self* as an entity capable of getting things done its way and using the individual to accomplish it.

In essence, Self easily becomes the master to every person who is not under the control of God's Holy Spirit, with the person becoming the slave. ($14.99; 206 pages, 978-0983700630)

In this commentary on Revelation, author Fred DeRuvo draws back the curtain on chapters five through twenty-two, presenting information in an easy-to-understand style, written for the average person. One thing is certain regarding the book of Revelation. Because of its prophetic nature, Christians will continue to debate aspects of it until such a time as we can know for certain. Either the things found within Revelation are yet to come to pass, and that alone will prove their veracity, or they will not come to *pass. Only time will tell.* ($18.00; 392 pages, 978-0977424498)

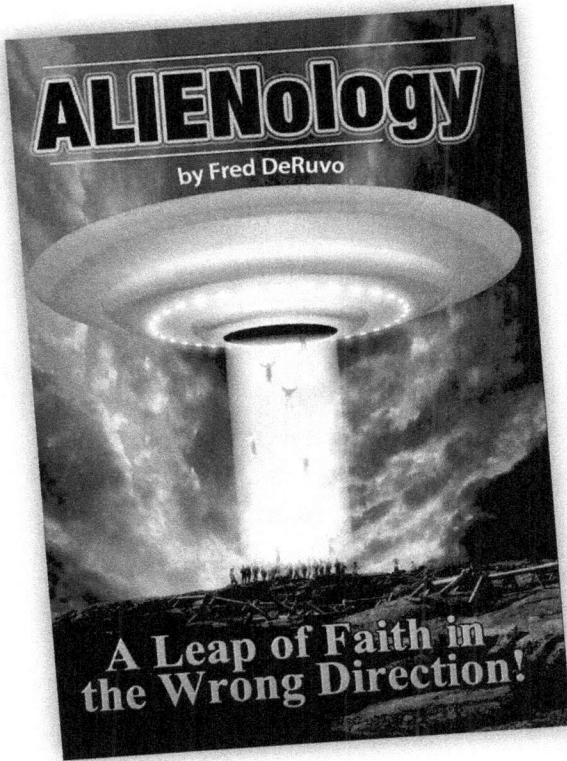

ALIENology
by Fred DeRuvo

A Leap of Faith in the Wrong Direction!

ALIENology is somewhat of a science for many who believe that entities from other planets or dimensions enter and leave our dimensions at will. What can we learn from these beings? Anything truthful? Dr. Fred believes that putting our faith in anything these beings say may be a huge leap in the wrong direction. Aliens reportedly come in all shapes, sizes, and even cultural representations. Because of this, there tends to be a good deal of mixed messages out there, yet people believe it because of their experience. Anything wrong with that picture? ($14.99; 176 pages, 978-0983700609)

Raised for His Glory delves into the books of Ezekiel and Romans to determine what the Bible actually says about Israel. Is the section on Ezekiel 36-39 speaking of a future time when nations will gather against Israel, or is this something that has already occurred? Moreover, just exactly what is the Valley of the Dry Bones referring to – the nation of Israel, or the Church? Join Dr. Fred as he presents his understanding of these very important sections of God's Word and how they relate to the only nation that He ever created, *Israel*. ($15.99; 190 pages, 978-0983700623)

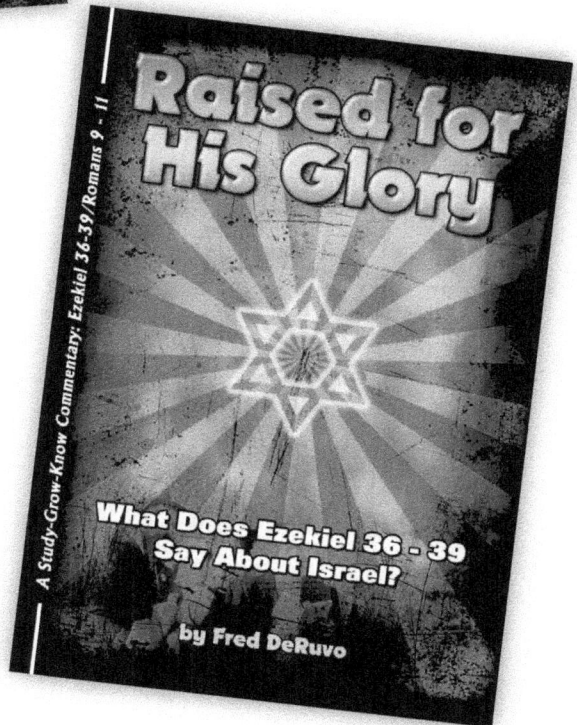

A Study-Grow-Know Commentary: Ezekiel 36-39; Romans 9 - 11

Raised for His Glory

What Does Ezekiel 36 - 39 Say About Israel?

by Fred DeRuvo

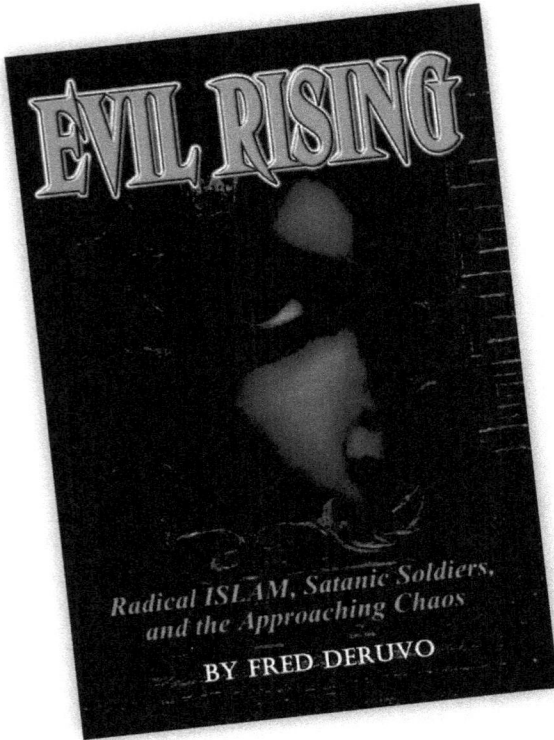

Radical ISLAM, Satanic Soldiers, and the Approaching Chaos
BY FRED DERUVO

There is a chaos coming that is predicated upon the rise of Islam, Satanic Soldiers, aliens, and evil beyond measure. As an ideology, Islam masquerades as a religious light to the world, one that promises to usher in world peace – but at what cost? Through the use of political strategies, military might, and religious tenets, adherents of Islam work within various established governments to create special laws or exemptions for Muslims in the hope of eventually overthrowing that established government. Can it happen? IS it happening? Find out in *Evil Rising*. ($13.95; 184 pages, 978-0977424429)

We hear all the time how bad things are getting throughout the world. Do we chalk it all up to being the normal cycles that occur in life, or is something else going on behind the scenes? What if this generation alive now turns out to be the last one before Jesus returns? Is there any truth at all to the claim that Jesus will return one day? If you are one who has not taken the time to read through some of the books of the Bible that are said to teach truths regarding the last days, *Living in the Last Generation* puts it out there in a straightforward manner, making it easy to understand. ($11.95; 132 pages. ISBN: 978-0977424405)

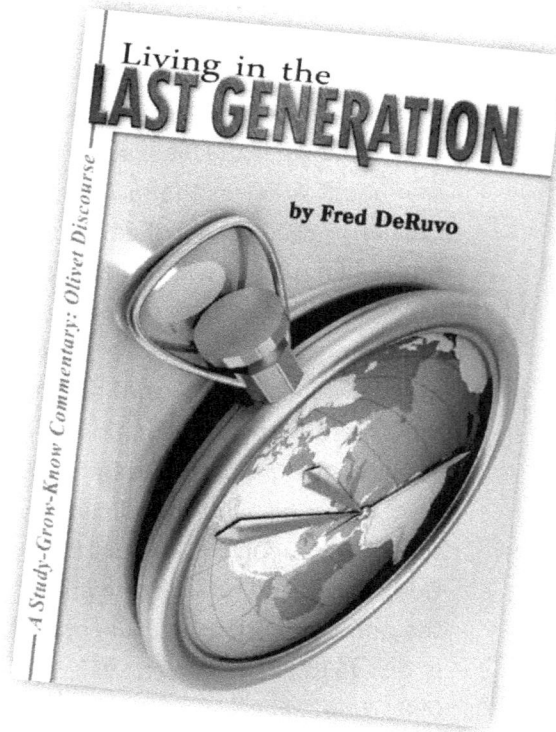

Living in the LAST GENERATION
by Fred DeRuvo
A Study-Grow-Know Commentary: Olivet Discourse

136

www.ingramcontent.com/pod-product-compliance
Lightning Source LLC
Chambersburg PA
CBHW081514040426
42447CB00013B/3221